LIBERATING THE BODY

LIBERATING THE BODY

Movements to Awaken Your Inner Self

TONY CRISP

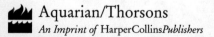
Aquarian/Thorsons
An Imprint of HarperCollins*Publishers*

The Aquarian Press
An Imprint of HarperCollins*Publishers*
77–85 Fulham Palace Road,
Hammersmith, London W6 8JB

Published by The Aquarian Press 1992
10 9 8 7 6 5 4 3 2 1

©Tony Crisp 1992

Tony Crisp asserts the moral right to
be identified as the author of this work

A catalogue record for this book
is available from the British Library

ISBN 1 85538 176 1

Typeset by Harper Phototypesetters Limited
Northampton, England
Printed in Great Britain by
Hartnolls Ltd, Bodmin, Cornwall

CONTENTS

Acknowledgements

My thanks to Erica Smith for real help, for the basic conception of this book, and for encouraging me to rewrite where necessary; Leon Crisp for talking over many of the ideas herein, and exploring inner-directed movement with me; John Hodgson, Jane Ribbens and Louise Winn for the moral support of trust; Yuzuru Katagiri, Denis Hoerner, and Hiroko Mizutani in Japan who joyously shared Seitai with me and taught me; Andrew, Barrie and Mike, my friends in Subud who have provided an environment in which I could explore the experience within their setting; Ti'Ko Computer Company for supplying such a first rate working tool, and Microsoft for a word processor – Word 5 – that did all I needed.

Introduction

Life Is Movement

While I was teaching relaxation I learnt that, when we truly relax, our bodies make spontaneous movements which express our own unique needs. This can be seen in yawning and stretching – movements which will not occur unless we feel at ease. From watching the people I worked with I came to understand that the quiet passivity we usually associate with relaxation is in fact only a small part of what the body wants to do to recharge. Spontaneous movements, if allowed, can develop into dynamic self-expression not only of the body, but also of voice and feelings. A wealth of unexpected possibilities can emerge: release of tension, unique exercises, healing of body and mind, and the development of your intuition are just a few examples.

Nothing in the realm of systematic exercises can compare with these spontaneous – or inner-directed – movements. They arise from our own unconscious knowledge of our personal and unique requirements, such as a need for physical stimulus in a sedentary job; for laughter and play if we are too serious; and for specific movements to mobilise stiff areas of the body or stimulate internal organs that are underactive. In particular, they appear to attempt a balancing and awakening of our beings to new levels of satisfying expression. Because such movements are not just empty physical activity, but combine and integrate body and mind, they bring about a healthier mental and emotional life.

The range of these spontaneous movements arising from our unconscious is difficult to believe unless you have experienced them. This is because most of us acknowledge only a tiny part of the creative potential we have. It is impossible to list all the aspects I have witnessed in people's self-expression. All movement and the feeling quality of movement is open to you when you begin to liberate your body in this way.

Chapter One

Secrets the Body Knows

The Beginnings of Inner-directed Movement

You already know the beginnings of how to relax enough to allow your body to make its own spontaneous movements. If you breathe in harmful dust your body makes the spontaneous movement of sneezing to protect the lungs and rid itself of the dust. Other similar movements are coughing, shivering when you are cold, and watering of your eyes. In these ways your body regulates and protects itself. But this is just the tip of the iceberg in regard to what you are capable of if you understand and learn to work with this process. It is the very edge of what you innately know about your own mental and physical needs and how to satisfy them.

It may seem strange to suggest that the process behind something as ordinary as yawning can have a potential to revolutionise the way you feel about yourself, can improve the mobility and well-being of your body and mind, and can reveal your intuition and creativity. But that is what I have witnessed in helping people use inner-directed movement. It shows you not only what your body needs to keep it functioning healthily, but also how to keep the feelings and mind mobile and healthy too. An intuitive function opens within yourself which can inform you wisely on important areas of your life.

This is understandable if certain facts are remembered. To grow physically and psychologically your being moves and directs itself from its own unconscious resources. You see this in everyday occurrences such as your heartbeat, digestive movements, perspiration, and even your ability to speak without searching for every word or worrying about what gestures you make. The important processes of your being, such as breathing, are nearly all expressed as inner-directed movement – that is, movements you do not have to consciously think about or copy from outside. They are movements which arise from your unconscious mental and physical life. All the gross and most subtle aspects of your life are expressed as movement. Laughter, crying, lovemaking are all powerful movements, largely inner-directed. Such movements integrate the different aspects of your self. For instance, love making is not just a physical activity, it also blends emotions, personal needs and deeper instinctive drives. In fact you, as a living being, are a master of expressive movement, but you may be holding yourself back.

Having no self-confidence doesn't remove your skill. I have discovered that even shy people, as they learn to relax deeply, have a world of splendid expressive movement inside them waiting to become known.

The organising principle that regulates the growth and shape of your body is expressed through inner-directed movement. It is the unconscious, self-regulating process of life. Its action continues working night and day. It is common to all of us, but few of us know how to work with it consciously to allow its magic to unfold more fully. This is possible through inner-directed movement.

In helping people to learn how to relax enough to allow such simple movements to extend into something fuller and more spontaneous, I witnessed people discovering the wide range of exercises, mimes and feelings their bodies could express unexpectedly. As people learnt to really relax they opened the door to abilities within their bodies and minds that had previously remained unconscious. This discovery was rather like dreaming of having lived in a house for years, only to find a door leading to a whole wing of the building which was previously unknown.

Inner-directed movement is:

1 A fuller expression of the natural power that regulates the body and mind. This can lead to physical and mental health.

2 An inbuilt and spontaneous urge to move and express the parts of oneself inhibited by the specialised environment of family, society or work. This is an urge toward wholeness, which is reached when concentration upon a limited area of yourself is relaxed, so that a greater symphony of expression between mind body and spirit occurs.

3 The creative and intuitive abilities of the mind. This is frequently experienced as spontaneous visualisation.

YOUR UNCONSCIOUS SOURCE OF LIFE AND GROWTH

To get a clearer picture of what it is you tap through inner-directed movement, it is helpful to imagine watching a film of your own development, like those showing speeded-up plant growth. If the film showed you from conception onwards, you would see amazing change and expansion. An extraordinary process would be seen causing your body and mind to unfold. You would observe incredible amounts of movement, many of them spontaneous. The movements in the womb, in babyhood and even in your adult sleep, are inner-directed and powerful. You would notice that, as you gradually mature, conscious control of movement becomes more prevalent. But still your sleep movements, breathing, yawning, stretching, laughter and tears keep you in touch with the incredibly wise process which directs your overall growth and survival. It is this often-forgotten, but very real process underlying your original growth and continued existence, that you contact when you relax fully.

> Inner-directed movements, occurring as they do when we relax deeply, arise from the unconscious processes that control our existence and growth. It is a fuller expression of what lies behind the growth of body and mind. It is what enables us to maintain a stable existence amidst the ever-moving forces of our environment. It holds all the systems of our being integrated in common purpose and is the foundation of consciousness. It is not something distant or separate from us, but is innately in everything we are and do.

FREEDOM TO BE YOURSELF

One of the first people who studied inner-directed movement with me was a woman in her sixties. Maria was married, had a lovely country cottage, but had not been outdoors for months. She was suffering from aches and pains in her arms, felt life had lost its interest, and asked for help. Maria quickly learned to relax enough to allow her body freedom to express itself without inhibiting self-criticism. Her movements were slow and tentative at first but soon included her whole body, producing feelings of pleasure. To allow such movements Maria had to learn how to give her body and feelings time in which to explore unplanned movement – movement arising from her own subtle body impulses. Such subtle urges are often overlooked or crowded out by thoughts of what one ought to be doing. So Maria created a mood, and gave herself time in which she could allow irrational movement – movement that had not been thought out beforehand or given by someone else. Such movements are usually quite different to the sort of things one finds recommended in exercise books. This is because they are often unique mixtures of exercise, dance, mime and generally letting oneself go enough to do what might otherwise be seen as ridiculous. Nevertheless, such irrational expression is very satisfying. In Maria's case she started with slow arm movements. Gradually the rest of her body was included in an expression of pleasure and sensual enjoyment in which she rolled and squirmed on the floor – movements and feelings that surprised Maria.

Within three weeks Maria went out with her husband and bought new clothes, something she hadn't done for years. She told me she realised she had been holding back all her pleasure, all her positive drive and feelings. In fact Maria had unconsciously been holding back HERSELF. In liberating her body and emotions she had liberated herself from the prison of her own depression.

The freedom and release which arise from inner-directed movement are also evident in what happened to Jim. An unmarried gas fitter, bored with his work and life, he joined a group using inner-directed movement. Within a couple of weeks Jim had learnt to give his body and feelings freedom to move. He was amazed at how fertile an imagination he had when he stopped holding himself back. His movements were creative and deeply felt. Less than two months had passed before Jim had given up his job and met the woman he would marry. Together they started working in a Steiner School for children.

Both of these examples show that inner-directed movement is basically a way of allowing what is already innate in oneself to be expressed more fully or easily. Put in the simplest of terms, by restraining the way you express yourself in movement and voice, you may be inhibiting important parts of your physical or psychological nature.

How Do You Learn Inner-directed Movement?

Learning inner-directed movement is in part learning how to drop your unconscious inhibitions and physical tensions. The first stages are a series of physical and mental exercises that help you to let your body, emotions and voice express themselves in ways you may previously have restrained because of social or personal expectations.

What Will Happen If I Really Let Go?

To learn anything new means treading new ground, opening yourself to new experience. This is certainly true of inner-directed movement. What you learn is largely something you experience rather than think. Because it involves movement it opens you to the realm of what you sense and perceive through body postures and feelings. This is an extraordinarily rich area, much overlooked in general schooling. In his book *The Turning Point* Fritjof Capra says, 'Retreating into our minds, we have forgotten how to "think" with our bodies, how to use them as agents of knowing.' Later, he says, we are led to see our body as a machine 'which is prone to constant failure unless supervised by doctors and treated with medication. The notion of the organism's inherent healing power is not communicated, and trust in one's own organism not promoted'.

This 'knowing' through your body and heart has many dimensions of experience. When my friends Sheila Johns, Mike Tanner and I first realised the possibilities of spontaneous movement in 1972, we created an environment in which we could explore it. This meant dropping our usual expectations of behaviour and allowing ourselves great freedom of possible self-expression. We took time to listen to how our bodies and emotions wanted to announce themselves. We let ourselves move in ways we had not previously conceived. We followed the usually unacknowledged impulses in our body and soul. I was amazed over and over again by what emerged from us.

One of my earliest experiences occurred when I was sitting quietly one day and my head began to move backwards. It was a gentle movement and I could have stopped it at any point. In fact I was so interested in it I tried to help it – tried to make it happen – and the movement stopped. Later, when I learnt to remain in a more relaxed state while my body moved, the spontaneous motion started again and my body re-enacted having my tonsils out as a six year old. Tensions had remained in my neck for all the years between six and thirty-four, and now that I had actually relaxed in the right way, my body could discharge the inner disturbance. Just prior to starting inner-directed movement my neck tension had got so bad that as I lay down to sleep at night my head pulled backwards painfully. After the release during inner-directed movement the pain never recurred.

Less specifically I remember that at first I would repeat really peculiar movements, what seemed an endless number of times. I felt that my body was working at freeing itself from habitual postures, attitudes and the results of past experience as well as massaging internal organs. Gradually my movements became freer and more mobile – although since my teens I had exercised and stretched regularly. Also the movements became mobility of my feelings as well as my body. For the first time in my life I realised that my soul, my psyche, had also been tense and stiff, and was being gently made more responsive, alive and whole.

On another occasion my body performed a forceful stamping dance in which I felt like a Japanese warrior. My voice also came into full play with such dances and movements. I need to stress that I had never danced before in my life, and I found such movements surprising.

Because of such encounters, and there were dozens of them, I felt I was allowing myself to experience something extraordinary. The experiences arising spontaneously from within created a sense of wonder in me. I recognised I was touching a secret which existed in everyone. The secret is that there is much more within us than we usually suspect. We are capable of more than we dare imagine, and have access to internal founts of healing, adventure, wisdom and experience that can enlarge and liberate us, not only physically but in our psyche as well. Our unconscious is full of creativity and splendid experience.

VOICE AS WELL AS BODY

As already suggested, the voice is also one of the important aspects of inner-directed movement. It is one of the areas of our life in which many inhibiting factors may occur. When sound and movement combine, as they do in this practice, a huge realm of experience and healing is possible. Joan, who attended an on-going group in Devon, described this as follows: 'Nothing else I have ever done is comparable to my experiences with inner-directed movement. When I began attending the group I honestly envied some people their ability to let go and say through their voices and bodies what was obviously deeply important to them and just as deeply satisfying. Seeing myself today I realise I have reached that sort of freedom and enjoyment.

'Friends ask me just what it is I do in the group. I just say I let my body express freely and they nearly always have a look of puzzlement. As far as they are concerned they already relax their body, but it doesn't dance or sing like mine. I don't even bother to explain as I know from experience they will not understand unless they do it themselves. All I know is that I have experienced all manner of magical things. I have felt the joyous abandonment of a baby and the fire of my body's power and sexuality. More than anything else, though, I have discovered I am a much wider and deeper person than I ever knew before.'

Because I have not simply been a teacher, but have practised inner-directed movement myself, I am just as much an enthusiast as Joan. I have no difficulty at all in being positive about what has come into my life from the practice. I look back from my mid-fifties, to when I began at thirty-four, and see that my body is far more mobile now. It is unbelievable to consider the attitudes and moral rigidity I lived with in my early thirties, and how tired I felt constantly, as well as depressed. The dark cloud I lived under, or in, has gone. Of course I had to meet some of the difficult emotions I had stored inside myself. Gradually 'blue sky' peeped through as the clouds I had unwittingly created in my life cleared. Also, because inner-directed movement puts you in touch with your creative centre, after twenty years I am still learning from the process.

LIBERATING THE BODY IS MORE THAN AVOIDANCE OF TENSION

Learning how to promote inner-directed movement is learning to trust yourself in a new way. It is also a way of learning how to use areas of your potential not previously employed, and to keep in contact with yourself and other people in a more enriching manner. But perhaps the most important fact about learning to allow inner-directed movement concerns liberation.

The difficulty is not in saying or being what is innately yourself, it is in doing so in a manner which does not conflict with the needs of others. The liberation you can find through inner-directed movement is very complete. It is not something you do to someone else or inflict on the world. It is yours to experience in your own physical and emotional privacy. Therefore, liberating your body through inner-directed movement releases reserves of energy and enthusiasm which might have been subdued by attempts to live within the boundaries of social or interpersonal demands. For many people, it is this enormous freedom which is the most important feature of the practice. Many people using inner-directed movement have told me they never before felt such freedom, even in childhood.

HOW DOES IT HAPPEN?

Earlier this century Dr Wilhelm Reich observed and wrote about the process of spontaneous movement during relaxation, becoming the father of modern body-oriented therapy. Adding to the basic biological statement that a function of life is movement he saw, for example, contraction, expansion and the sexual pelvic action as fundamental life movements, connected with personal wholeness. He found that if they were inhibited, frustration or illness of some sort resulted. But his work was still prior to the publication of information arising from research into sleep and dreams, which has thrown such extraordinary light on how our bodies and minds work together. In particular, the observation that our eyes always move rapidly whilst we are dreaming gives insight into how movements can arise without our consciously attempting them. The brain produces all the impulses for our muscles that it would during waking activity, so inner-directed movement may be arising from the same source as our dreams. I make this connection because the powerful mimes and experiences have an intensity and reality akin to dreams. Inner-directed movement and dreams arise out of a relaxed condition. Both produce spontaneous movements and dramatic experience or fantasy.

Laboratory tests in which subjects were prevented from dreaming show that those tested developed symptoms of great stress and decreased mental efficiency. The conclusion was that the process underlying dreaming is of critical importance in keeping the mind and body functioning properly. If we remember that dreams do this by releasing spontaneous drama, movement and emotions, then the spontaneity of inner-directed movement can be seen as linking with the important release and balancing action of the dream process.

The evidence showing dreaming as critical to mental and physical health suggests that dreams may be a last ditch stand against the inhibition of some of the most important aspects of yourself. There may therefore be a connection between the expression of subtle needs and emotions in dreams, and the uninhibited expression of your body and feelings during inner-directed movement. People also find that inner-directed movement enhances their personal growth and intuition.

The Experience of Inner-directed Movement

A female student once said to me, 'I have relaxed thousands of times and no unwilled movements have happened, so why will it be different this time?' She went on to say, 'I don't believe there is anything in me to create the sort of experience you are talking about anyway!'

Her question and statement have behind them viewpoints and attitudes that in fact make it difficult to understand just what inner-directed movement is, and how it can happen. Nevertheless, laboratory tests have shown that the most materialistic people, while they are in the relaxed state of sleep, develop spontaneous fantasies, accompanied by body movements, emotions and speech. Namely they dream, even if they do not remember. The spontaneous movements we make in sleep, and the deeply moving feelings and dramas we experience in connection with them, are usually not strong enough to break through to conscious life except in a few cases. To work with this process, which is vital to your well-being, you need to be receptive and create the right mood and environment. The body and mind are not disconnected. The wisdom that keeps the body heat at the correct level, the intelligence that keeps millions of various cells interacting in an integrated way, though unconscious, unknown, untouched by yourself in everyday life, can begin to bubble up into awareness and self-realisation when you let it express itself in its own way.

That is the theory. The experience is that if you do take time to let this subtle action have a space in waking life, you must first learn to let your body be free enough to move to delicate impulses. As the movements strengthen through learning to trust yourself in letting go, they will follow certain themes. Perhaps at the end of the session you will see your body has been exercising and loosening, or making dance-like movements on a theme such as emerging from restrictions and growing. You may find that this relates to how you feel in everyday life. You will see that the creative imagination of dream life is clarified and showing itself to you while you are awake.

It's an Old Truth in a New Form

The view that you do not need to practise disciplined or energetic exercises to keep physically and psychologically healthy may be new to you. Everything, from PE at school to aerobics and yoga, suggests series of given movements or postures which one must perform correctly in order to benefit. However, inner-directed movement is not a new practice. Because it is a basic human function, and an extension of movements like yawning, it has been used frequently in the past. In fact it has a history of many thousands of years, different cultures giving it different names and explanations.

While I was teaching inner-directed movement in Japan I was

introduced to an almost identical practice called Seitai. The founder of Seitai, Haruchika Noguchi, is said to have modernised an older practice which was a part of Buddhist traditional technique.

I had the pleasure of meeting several Seitai practitioners who taught me their approach to inner-directed movement. My wife Hyone and I were also able to attend group practices. Seitai is very popular in Japan, and its practitioners come from a wide age range and are equally represented by both sexes. The on-going group we attended had about thirty members. There were teenagers, married couples, young and old, and lots of single people.

Seitai's appeal is probably due to Noguchi's practical and down-to-earth approach. Many people in Japan have improved their physical and psychological health using this very simple practice. In the following chapters some of Seitai's approaches will be explained.

In India the use of inner-directed movement is called Shaktipat. It has a different approach to that of Seitai, contact with a teacher or Guru being recommended though not indispensable. Individuals in most of these approaches practise both alone or in groups.

While working in Australia I was told by Jack Thompson, who had been taught Tai Chi by a Chinese teacher, that for three years he had been instructed to perform specific given movements. Then, one day, he said to Jack, 'Now I will show you the real Tai Chi'. From that moment, he encouraged Jack to allow spontaneous movement – inner-directed movement.

Tai Chi is a stylised series of movements from China used for health and for harmonising one's being. While in Hong Kong I saw hundreds of people in the early morning practising Tai Chi in Kowloon Park. Hyone and I joined in and it was a great pleasure to have the freedom to openly explore movement in public. Also originating in China there is a more direct approach to spontaneous movement called Qi Gong. As in Seitai the individual or group directly waits for spontaneous movement.

These Eastern approaches see the movements as expressing a subtle energy called Chi or Ki, the creative, body-forming energy of life. The practice is considered to balance and harmonise the way this energy is expressed in oneself.

The West also has its traditional approaches to inner-directed movement. Apart from groups such as the Quakers and Shakers, who gave inner-direction a religious orientation connected with the spontaneous movements of the original Pentecost, Anton Mesmer founded a form of group practice 300 years ago. He was probably one of the first to attempt a scientific evaluation of the process. Without the recent findings which have arisen from psychological and neurological research, however, his explanations were based on even older ideas.

Ancient tribal healing or decision-making frequently involved spontaneous movements and vocal expression. These are often linked to what is known to us as shamanism, a way in which ancient people found wholeness and healing, or sought intuitive information vital to their existence.

A more recent practice that started in Indonesia is called Subud. It has a format that has allowed it to become popular worldwide although, unlike Seitai, it has an element of religious feeling because of the culture and character of its founder, Pak Subuh. In Subud, groups of people meet twice a week. Someone in the group says, 'Begin', and the members allow spontaneous expression of body and voice.

Although all these approaches have a very similar core in that practitioners are asked to let go of self-willed activity, the explanations of the practice and the details may vary. For instance, in Seitai there is not very much vocal expression. The men, women and children can all practise together, and there is no religious connection. In Subud the men and women are segregated. There is a lot of vocal expression, and there is a cultural religious connection.

THE BEST OF SELF-HELP AND SPIRITUAL ADVENTURE

The techniques described in the following pages have been developed from an acquaintance with approaches used in the past by other cultures, from study and practice of traditional and recent Western methods, and from my own twenty years of experience of personal use and teaching inner-directed movement internationally. From this I know that the aims of self-help and self-responsible health, aimed at by alternative forms of healing, are available through inner-directed movement. I find the practice combines the energy balancing of acupuncture, the release and personal growth of psychotherapy, and the inner adventure of meditation or dream work.

Chapter Two

LETTING YOUR BODY SPEAK

Spontaneous movement was natural to us as babies. We moved our arms and legs in ways that would develop muscles, express feelings and stimulate growth. Our emotions were vented directly and powerfully through such movements. We cried when upset, laughed when happy, and when the time was right we practised all manner of sounds in preparation for speech. All this without the intervention of any planning or list of exercises to do. In this way we maintained our physical and psychological health. In a similar unselfconscious manner we were able to traverse formidable stages of physical and psychological growth.

Without formal lessons or given exercises we practised what was new from an inner-directed source. We quickly learned the lessons of language and walking and persisted despite many failures. Without boredom we practised the same movements and sounds endlessly until we were capable in them and could move on to extended skills. We took in the cultural and grammatical information around us and put it to work. We found order in the chaos of the mass of information presented to us. Even as babies our bodies and minds were incredibly resourceful in their own right without formal tuition. Nearly all of this occurred because we were letting ourselves react spontaneously in response to our environment.

REGAINING YOUTHFUL ABILITIES

Learning inner-directed movement is relearning how to trust our own innate capability and power again; to trust the life-enhancing drives we felt in childhood; to trust the subtle urges of our bodies to move and feel, urges arising from the unconscious centre from which growth and life emerged. Trust, because it takes self-reliance to allow the new, the previously unknown and unplanned to emerge and be felt. We must learn to let ourselves play and move without the deadening self-criticism that can cripple expression in adult life. We must also learn in some degree to stand outside the social conditioning acquired as we were growing up.

Learning to allow the same inner-directed movement and mental learning that operated in early childhood is not done to replace our hard-won conscious will or our reasoning and decision-making. The more instinctive or intuitive source of growth and learning promotion that operated in childhood is a great addition to conscious will, not a replacement. In fact, when the rational mind acts in a cooperative and monitoring way with the unconscious or intuitive self, a much greater efficiency occurs in both.

Through this cooperation we access resources that can lead to greater health, and an improvement in the functioning of the immune system. We can also meet our own creativity in a degree usually only glimpsed in the adventure and strangeness of dreams. One of the most significant aspects of inner-directed movement, however, is its ability to continue the action of psychological growth into greater maturity and freedom.

Letting go and allowing one's being to fulfil its own spontaneous needs is a thing of great simplicity. It is easy. It takes no effort or thought at all. It is even easier than attempting to relax. But because we habitually believe we must always decide or will what to do – the feeling that nothing will happen unless we do it – it may take time to learn how to let go in a way that allows action. In Eastern practices this is called action in non-action. It is helpful to think of it as holding yourself in a condition of sensitive balance, like the keys on a piano. A touch on a piano key causes it to move and the note to play, but as soon as the finger is removed the key springs back into place ready to move again if necessary. The difference between the piano key being moved and the action of inner-directed movement is that no external finger or force motivates you. The same sort of subtle but persuasive impulses that move our chests in breathing are allowed to flow into action and feeling.

If there is anything to be learnt, it is how to feel and allow the flow and movement of these life impulses – to let them lead to unanticipated and creative movement and self-expression. You will learn to meet and melt the subtle resistances which cause you to hold back from wholeness, from more self-awareness. It is therefore helpful to explore and respond to some of these subtle feelings in yourself before attempting the full freedom of inner-directed movement.

LIBERATING THE BODY – PHASE ONE

WARM-UP AND LOOSENING MOVEMENTS

It is useful, at least in the early days of learning inner-directed movement, to warm up your body. Some helpful movements will be outlined later.

The series of movements was arrived at in a special way. After I had learnt to allow inner-directed movement, and my body and mind felt expressive in it, I found the spontaneous movements would respond to a question. For example, if I had a dream that puzzled me, I could ask what a particular figure in it represented, and my body would respond spontaneously in a descriptive mime. Because the information the mime presented often added to what I knew consciously, I felt the 'answer' that arose through movement was expressing unconscious insights.

One day I was experimenting with this question and response, and asked what would be a helpful way to bring the body and mind to harmony. I was astonished as an extremely long and detailed response flowed spontaneously from me. Movement after movement arose apparently from my unconscious, along with an understanding of how the movements influenced basic biological and psychological processes such as introversion and extroversion of energy and awareness. As I used these movements, I realised they are not simply exercises to make the body active and stimulated. For instance, if I cannot breathe properly I am not functioning well. If my hips are locked in tension and my pelvis cannot express tender sexual feelings, or if my abdomen is tight and my internal organs cannot digest food properly, then the basic urges of life are being interfered with. The exercises loosen the body in a way that allows a fuller expression of these basic life-movements – such as the expansion and contraction of the chest in relationship to the spine; the swinging pelvis expressing sexuality and its connection with the chest, neck and head. Tensions restricting the way life-processes are expressed in movements such as breathing lie at the root of much physical and psychological illness.

The following movements are those I learnt that day. If you enjoy them and have time, by all means do the movements consecutively. They are excellent for health in themselves, but they are not inner-directed movement. They are given to warm your body and help mobilisation and internal balancing.

Use these movements at least three times over a period of a week or so, before going on to the next phase. Practise each movement for between one and three minutes, depending on your energy and time. Try doing them with music sometime to see if it aids the good feelings they can produce. Later suggestions for types of music are given in detail. At this point something fairly flowing without too much drama in it.

These are only warm-up movements, they are not inner-directed movement. Inner-directed movement, once learnt, can be used easily and for a few minutes. There is not a long list of 'movements' to use in the proper practice, although there are a variety of ways you can use it.

It is helpful to 'meditate' on some of the movements after performing them. This means that you try to recreate the feeling or sensation of the movement again without allowing your body to make the movement. The idea is to exercise your inner awareness and feelings of energy movement. So in the third movement, the pelvic swing, you would create the feeling of the hips pushing forward and up, followed by the pulling back and down of the pelvis. This meditation exercise is important as it enables you to gain some control of your inner feelings. Often such feelings are stimulated by external events or unconscious worries. Your meditation is harmonising and balancing these feelings.

These movements take time, so if you are not able to do them all in sequence, do those you can within the time available and work through the other movements during future sessions. You need a reasonable space – something at least the size of a single blanket, so you can feel free to move without bumping into things.

Squatting And Rising

When you get used to the movement, going down into the squat position should be done fairly fast with the out-breath quite strong so there is an audible blowing of air out of the lungs. It can be done gently, but if possible, do it strongly as the body drops. Let the hips go down as far as you comfortably can, and let the head fall down too so the body is relaxed. You may need to put your heels on a couple of similar-sized books to make squatting comfortable. The hands come forward in a scything movement until they meet just above the dropped head. If you cannot squat low enough, use a stool or chair to sit on as you go down, so that you only drop a short way.

At least two feeling states are involved in this movement. One is the standing erect and 'open' feeling. The other is the down, closed and relaxed feeling. When you feel fluid in the movement see if you can enhance these feeling changes as you move between the opposites of up and down. While down feel the relaxed letting-go feeling. While up feel the active, energetic feeling.

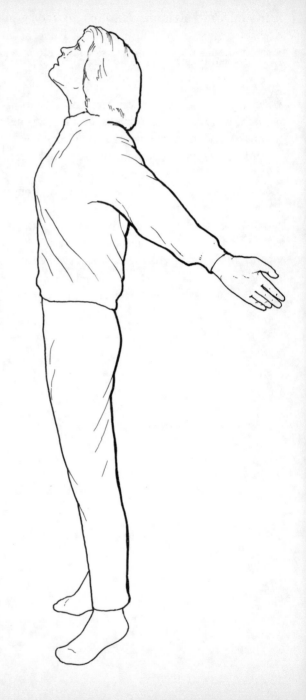

1 In this first movement, start from a standing position, with feet slightly apart.

2 Take an in-breath, and as you reach the high point of inhalation take your head and arms slightly backwards to widen the chest.

3 From the standing position begin to breathe out and bend the knees so that you can drop into a squat. Let your arms move forward and up so the hands come palms together near to the face and expel your breath while dropping into the squatting position.

4 At this point you should be squatting with head relaxed forward.
Rest there for a moment and then carry on the movement by
breathing in and rising back to the first position again. To do this,
you should slowly stand as you breathe in, expanding the rib cage
again by opening the arms slightly backwards and apart, letting the
head drop back.

5 Repeat the cycle of squatting and rising in your own time.

6 Now 'meditate' on the movement for about a minute. This means
standing or sitting with eyes closed and imagining doing the
movement, but hardly moving your body. Try to reproduce the
feelings of the movement. Feel the relaxed, down condition, then

move into the up, dynamic feeling. This is an important exercise in becoming aware of the subtle feelings connected with movement, and learning to mobilise them.

Circling The Hips

To get the movement satisfyingly mobile, it is helpful to imagine yourself standing in the middle of a large barrel. The aim is then to run your hips around the inside of the barrel, touching it all the way around. This helps to get the full circling of the pelvis. So, as the hips are circling back the trunk is bent slightly forward, but still with the head high. The hips should go well out to the side, and as they swing to the front they should be far forward enough to cause the trunk to be inclined slightly backwards. If you cannot manage this at first, simply do what you can.

The knees and ankles should be kept relaxed, as should the hips themselves, so they adapt to the circling. The breathing should then also find its own rhythm: generally it is out as the hips swing forward, and in as they swing backwards. This is because the chest is slightly compressed as the hips are forward and the head is floating erect.

1 Begin from a standing position as in the first exercise, but with feet slightly farther apart, about shoulder width.

2 Keeping your head and shoulders more or less floating in the same position, circle the hips horizontally. The pelvis is taken gradually into a wide circle.

3 Repeat the movement in the opposite direction for the second half of the exercise.

4 Meditate on the movement for about one minute. You can stand or sit to do this.

Pelvic Swing

If you imagine a vertical circle – seen from one side of your body – and move the hips around it fluidly while letting the legs and trunk follow, that is the movement. Although simple this is an important movement as far as becoming aware of the subtler side of your own being is concerned.

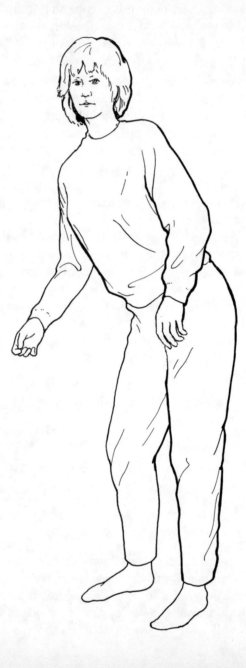

The movement is similar to the backward and forward movement of sexual intercourse, except that it is circular and involves bending and straightening the legs. But it does still involve the pelvis swinging backward and forward. Do the movement until you can feel your body loosening and flowing more easily. Then, repeat the movement slowly, being aware of the different feelings of the pelvis as it points forward and backward. These feelings are quite subtle, but are strong enough to be easily noticed if the movement is done with awareness of the change.

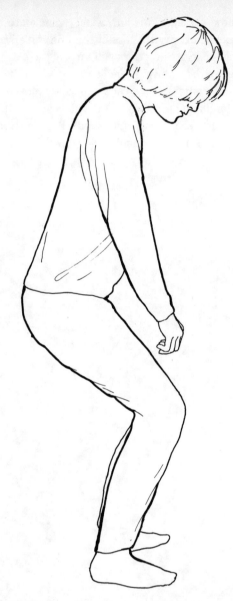

1 Standing with your feet about a foot apart, move your pelvis
   backwards – as if starting to sit down – to begin a circle. This half-
   sitting position inclines the head and trunk forward and bends the
   knees slightly.

2 Start to push the hips well forward, to the point where the trunk
 is inclined backwards. As you do so the knees are straightened

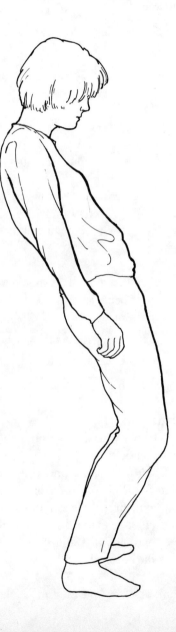

again, and this completes the full circle with the hips in a way that describes or 'draws' a vertical circle. If the hips are not taken well back in the starting position, or well forward in this second position, the circle is 'flattened'.

3 Do the movement in a way that keeps the hips swinging in the circle in a continuous flow.

4 Meditate on the movement while sitting or standing.

Roller Skating

If possible let most of the movement occur from below the navel. You can keep your eyes looking ahead, with your arms swinging in time with the hips to let the body move fully. But it is the lower back that is being worked here. Do the movement fairly vigorously. This movement massages the lower internal organs as well, so you may get a 'stitch' until you adapt to the exercise. If this does happen, don't stop altogether, just slow down. The movement will then massage the area of discomfort.

1 Stand with your feet a little wider than shoulder width, with trunk bent forward and knees bent also. Your back should be reasonably straight although at an incline.

2 Now swing the hips from side to side, making the lowest part of the spine alternate to the left and right.

3 Now meditate on the movement.

Swinging The Trunk

Be careful to check whether your feet slip on the floor surface. If you cannot easily maintain a feet-wide position, it may help to stand with bare feet. The movement is an active one, with a light pause as you reach top and bottom. Some people like to allow their arms to extend in a wide arc as they come up, as it feels more balanced. Also, as you come to the upright position with the in-breath, let the head drop back slightly, and arms extend sideways and back to increase the chest stretch. This balances the deep exhalation accomplished by dropping the trunk forward.

Swinging the Trunk is a very pleasing movement, and because it

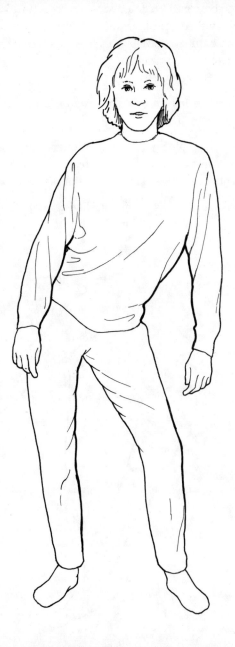

connects with the breath cycle, it develops a particular rhythm. If you can manage it without becoming giddy, let the exhalation of breath as you go down be quite energetic.

1 Stand with the feet about twice shoulder width.

2 Let your head and trunk drop forward and the arms hang relaxed, allowing the spine to be gently stretched.

3 When you feel your spine has adapted to the position, swing your head and trunk to the left on an out-breath, allowing your body to roll over and up to the standing position as you breathe in.

4 Drop the trunk downwards in the mid-line again, breathing out – do it fairly fast – then roll head and trunk to the right as you come up and breathe in again.

5 Continue the cycle with a slight pause at the high and low of each swing.

6 Meditate on the movement, reproducing the relaxed drooping feeling and the active, 'up' feeling.

Surrendering Backwards

This movement works the abdominal muscles quite strongly, and needs to be approached slowly until you feel confident and able in it. It is not primarily a physical exercise. The aim of the movement is not to see how far backward you can go: it is to express the feeling of letting go of self, of dropping control in a disciplined way. At first, when the head and shoulders are back, hold the position for a very short time, then recover to the upright stance. As you get used to the movement, you can stay in the surrendered position longer – just as long as is comfortable – then recover.

1 Start with feet about shoulder width apart. On an in-breath, drop your head slowly back and breathe out, allowing your head, shoulders and trunk to drop slightly backwards with the arms limp.

2 If you are comfortable, breathe as normally as you can while your trunk is backwards.

3 Hold for a short time then return to the upright position.

4 Repeat several times.

5 Meditate on the movement, between the surrendered feeling and the taking-control, upright feeling.

Sideways Lunge

This movement makes greater use of the legs and introduces more spinal twist. Because you are reaching forward with the opposite hand to the bent knee, there is a common tendency for people to extend the whole trunk forward too, and that is unnecessary. The trunk curves upright from the trailing leg. The breathing sequence for this is out as you lunge, in as you centre again.

When you are reasonably capable at the movement try doing it as slowly as possible. Make the breath slow, and move in time with the out-breath as you lunge and the in-breath as you centre. This is a very powerful movement so don't attempt too many repetitions at first.

1 Start with feet about a metre apart in a standing position, with the hands palms together in front of the chest.

2 Turn the right foot to point to the right and turn the trunk to face in that direction also.

3 Let the right knee bend until the hips drop right down near the right heel. Meanwhile the left leg is trailing, forming a curve from the floor up along the spine. The left knee is on the floor but hardly bent. To make this easier, let the right heel rise if necessary.

4 As you lunge to the right, let the left hand stretch forward in the

direction you are lunging. The right arm stretches back towards the left foot. This gives a slight spinal twist.

5 From the lunge position, using the strength of the right leg, push back into the upright position until the trunk faces forward, and bring the hands back to the centred position in front of the chest.

6 Repeat the exercise to the left. Don't forget that it is now the right arm you extend forward – always the opposite hand.

7 With a slight pause at each lunge, and while 'centred', repeat the movement alternatively to left and right.

8 Meditate on the movement, remembering to get the 'centred', poised feeling between each imagined lunge.

Spinal Twist

This is more of a spinal twist than the last movement. The arms describe a wide arc, and come to rest where you feel comfortable, but not floppy. The breath cycle is to complete exhalation as the spinal twist is completed, and to complete inhalation as you reach midpoint between the left and right twist. Like the previous exercise, if the breathing is united with the movement, it makes for a more satisfying experience. Once you have got the feel for integrating breathing and movement, perform this one fairly slowly and purposefully.

1 Stand with feet a little wider than shoulder width, hands at your sides.

2 Leading with the head, turn to the left, lifting your arms and letting them describe a wide circle, and continuing their movement when head and trunk can turn no further. As the trunk turns to the left, let the feet and knees accommodate the twist so that, when you have turned as far as you can to the left, your left knee is slightly bent in a semi-lunge to allow the fullest twist, and your foot is pointing to the left.

3 Turn from there to the right, going round as far as you can, fairly slowly to let the feet and legs change.

4 Continue this slow swing, making sure you allow a semi-lunge at the end of each swing to give a little more twist.

5 Meditate on the movement.

The Swinging Ribcage

This exercise aims at mobilising the ribcage in a movement it seldom gets the chance to make in everyday life. To make sure your ribcage is actually doing what it should, it is helpful at first to practise in front of a mirror. Keeping the hips still and the ribcage centred, hold your index fingers about two inches away from each side of your lower ribs. Now see if you can swing the ribs sideways towards the extended but still finger without swaying the whole trunk and hips sideways as well. At first it might be that you do not know just what muscles to move to accomplish this, but with practice it becomes simple.

Like one of the earlier movements, this one may cause you to develop a 'stitch' if you do it fairly actively. This is because it strongly massages the internal organs, and this is a healthy stimulus for them. It may also cause an unusual bellows action with the lungs, causing a pumping of air in and out of the lungs without actually breathing. This is quite normal for the movement, and is not harmful. No need to meditate this one.

1 Keeping the hips still, swing the lower ribs slightly sideways. If you do this with the right side of the ribcage, it causes the left shoulder to drop, and the right to rise. When you alternately swing to the right and left, the shoulders alternately rise and fall also.

2 If you lift and drop the shoulders alternately, this may extend the ribcage, but not necessarily so. Many people move their shoulders thus, or swing their hips energetically, without their ribcage being mobilised at all.

3 Swing left and right until you can do the movement easily.

The Crawl

Your attention has been moving up the body in this series of exercises, so you are now concentrating more on the chest and shoulders. This exercise primarily mobilises the shoulders and ribcage in relation to the spine, but it also brings the arms into action in more than a supporting role.

It helps if you imagine the hands are pulling backwards through water. Meanwhile, the head and hips should remain facing forward, so the shoulders swing around the steady spine. The movement can be done slowly but strongly, or fast and energetically. This is a wonderful movement to massage neck and lungs.

1 Stand with feet about shoulder width apart.

2 Be aware of the knees and keep them very slightly bent and relaxed.

3 Keeping your head and hips still, make the swimming movements of the 'crawl' with your arms. This means the right arm swings up and forward above the head as the left arm is low and moving

backwards. Then the left arm is up and forward as the right drops. The movement is a slow circling of the arms.

5 Finish with the still meditation of the movement.

The Breath Meditation

This is more of a meditation than an exercise, but is important in mobilising the inner feelings that lie behind movements. When you begin this meditation, do not be in a hurry to open your hands to

let the feeling of pleasure radiate out. In fact, let the hands be as spontaneous as possible in expressing what you feel. It may be that your hands thereby move a great deal, or very little. If there is an urge to move the hands in other ways than suggested, then you should allow this to happen.

1 Stand in a comfortable, balanced position with the hands in front of the chest, palms together and eyes closed.

2 Imagine that, as you breathe in, the air is fanning a small glowing

coal inside the chest. The incoming air makes the coal glow gently. This coal is just a symbol of the subtle pleasure sensations generated by slow, purposeful inhalation. If you can be directly aware of this pleasure, dispense with the image of the coal.

3 Let the hands indicate the amount of this glow or pleasure. Let them do this by moving apart, so that if the pleasure is intense the hands reach wide. As you exhale and the glow fades, let the hands come together. If there is little felt, then the hands should remain unopened.

Playing With The Voice

If you have lots of time you can use this after the warming-up movements. Otherwise use it by itself, taking up to fifteen minutes. It may help to use music as a background, although it should be something which is not too invading.

In this exercise you explore the use of sound. To make different sounds you need to move not only your throat, but also your trunk and even limbs in different ways. Sounds also evoke feelings and move or exercise them. Just as many of us do not move our bodies outside of certain restricted and habitual gestures and actions, so also your range of sounds may be quite small. For several minutes you will explore making sounds.

As your sound production improves and you begin to enjoy it, explore making all sorts of happy sounds in different sessions: different sorts of laughter; angry noises; animal and bird noises; sensual sounds; the sound of crying or sobbing; natural sounds such as wind, water, earthquakes; make the sounds of different languages and different situations such as a warrior's chant, a mother's lullaby (without real words, just evocative sounds), a lover's song, a hymn to Life, or even sounds about birth and death; and just plain nonsense noises. Don't attempt to explore all these different types of sound at one session. Just choose one and explore it until you can feel yourself limbering up in it and getting past restricting feelings such as shyness or stupidity. Those are the walls of restriction.

1 Start by taking a full breath and letting it out noisily with an AHHHH sound.

2 Do this until you feel it resonating in your body. This may take one or two minutes.

3 Change to a strong EEEEEE sound. Once more, continue for at least a minute.

3 Now try MMMMMAAAAA.

4 If you are doing this exercise for the first time, that is sufficient for one session. If not, go on to use one of the themes suggested above.

The Yawning Exercise

Do not use this exercise until you have used the warm-up and loosening movements a few times, as well as the voice exercise.

One of the easiest ways to begin inner-directed movement is to use your body's own urge to express spontaneous movement, as with yawning. To do this, take time to create the right setting for the practice. Play some music that is flowing, but without a strong beat. A strong rhythm grabs the body and feelings too much and so prevents creativity in your expression. Most of Kitaro's music is useful for this. Try also *Moods*, a collection of modern mood music, most of Enya's music, *Meditation* by Thais, and some of the Vangelis albums. Music also 'gives permission' for easier self-expression, as you are less worried about making a noise or moving.

Do not go on to the other exercises described after the yawning exercise. Practise this one a few times on different days before attempting the next ones.

You need clothes suitable for easy movement, and about ten to twenty minutes during which you can give yourself fully to whatever your body and feelings suggest. Do not take this suggestion of time rigidly, though. If your session is shorter or longer, follow your own needs.

1 When ready, stand in the space, listen to the music and drop unnecessary tensions. Remind yourself that for the next few minutes you are going to let your body play. You are going to let it off the lead.

2 Open your mouth wide with head slightly dropped back and simulate yawning. As you do so, notice whether a natural yawn

starts to make itself felt. If it does, allow it to take over and have a really luxurious yawn. Any following impulse to yawn again should be allowed.

3 Let the yawns come one after the other if they want to. Without acting it out, let the impulse to yawn take over your body, not just your mouth and face. So if the urge to move includes the arms or elsewhere, let it happen.

4 Give yourself over to the enjoyment of having time to really indulge your own natural feelings and body pleasure. If the yawning develops into other movements and stretches, let it. In the same way you would normally allow your body to express itself in a yawn, let it express itself in whatever other form of movement, postures or stretches arise. Maybe it will be noisy yawns, so allow whatever noises you want to make, however 'silly'. If this flows into movements following the music, don't hold yourself back, although your movements might not follow the music, but have a direction of their own. This is playtime with your body, so enjoy it. What has gone before has simply been preparatory. Now you can do what you want.

5 Until you feel ready to stop, simply enjoy or explore the movements and feelings that arise – even if what arises for you after the initial yawns is a desire to lie on the floor and rest. That also is you expressing your needs.

The yawning exercise is an excellent way to release tensions, especially those of the neck and face. It is also the beginning of inner-directed movement.

Fiona, a woman who allowed herself this liberation of the body for the first time, describes her experience as follows:

I found a quiet moment, spread a rug on the floor, knelt down with my head touching my knees and started running my hands through my hair – I have always found this very comforting. Soon I noticed myself beginning to wobble and shake, and it seemed so funny I began to laugh. I laughed without stopping for twenty minutes, rolling about the floor, on my face; on my back kicking my legs in the air; on my knees beating my hands on the floor. The tears rolled down my face, my voice became cracked, my diaphragm began to ache with unaccustomed exercise and still I went on laughing. Eventually I ended up by going round and round on the rug on my knees and elbows, banging my elbows on the floor in joyous abandon, my head and arms muffled up in my jersey which had slipped off me at some time, singing a wordless song of joy and freedom. Absolutely nothing mattered.

Experiencing Your Body's Magic – The Relaxed Arm Test

This interesting test helps you to experience the sensation of inner-directed movement in a playful way. Try it with your friends.

It is important to let go of effort and allow your body to have the 'piano key' poise when you relax your arm at the end of the experiment.

1 Stand about a foot away from a wall, side on, so your right hand is near to a clear space on the wall.

2 Lift your right arm sideways, keeping it straight, until the back of your hand is against the wall. Because you are near to the wall and your arm is straight you will only manage to lift your arm part of the way. So when the back of your hand touches the wall, press it hard against the wall as if trying to complete the movement of lifting your arm.

3 Do not press the hand against the wall by leaning, but by keeping the arm straight and trying to complete the lifting motion. Using a reasonable amount of effort stay with the hand pressing against the wall for about twenty seconds.

4 Now move so that you face away from the wall and with eyes closed, relax and be aware of what happens.

5 Try the experiment a couple of times with each arm before reading the next paragraph.

What you have done is to attempt a movement. Because the wall prevented this, the body was not able to complete the movement you asked it to make, building up a muscular *charge* in your shoulder (deltoid) muscle. When you stepped away from the wall, the arm, if relaxed, was free to complete the movement. So your arm may have risen from your side as if weightless, thus discharging its energy. Some people need several tries before they can find the right body feeling to allow the arm its movement. It is easy to prevent it moving because the impulse is quite a subtle one.

This technique enables you to learn how to give your body freedom to move under its own impulse. The way your arm moved, and the experience of an unwilled movement, is very similar to inner-directed movement, and is also an example of how the body self-regulates through spontaneous movement. It is therefore helpful either to practise the technique until you can do it, or use it a number of times to establish your relationship with the feeling of it. The sense of allowing movement can then be used in inner-directed movement itself.

It would be quite helpful to practise this experiment a few times before moving on to the next.

LIBERATING THE BODY – PHASE TWO

In *Phase One* you began to learn the process of permitting your body to move in a way that allowed it more freedom of expression. Now this will be extended to showing the beginnings of your own creativity.

Once more, create an open space for yourself in which to allow not only freedom of movement, but also freedom to express yourself. The space is both physical and mental. You need to have enough space to stand or lie on – a space about the size of a single blanket is the minimum possible. If you have more available space, though, use it. Clear it of objects you might bump into, as you might like to practise with your eyes closed. Remove jewellery that might get caught or broken by free movement. Wear clothes – or be without clothes – allowing you to feel unrestricted.

CREATING THE RIGHT SETTING

The mental space you create for yourself might be even more important than the physical. This is because just physical space is not enough. You must be able to give yourself permission to express freely with your body, your feelings, and your voice. The restrictions in your mental space might be obstacles, such as wanting to know what it is you are going to do before you let yourself do it; worrying about what someone might think if they knew or could hear what you are doing; the feeling that there is nothing worthwhile in you to emerge anyway, so you are just acting the fool.

A man who had just started exploring inner-directed movement, explained to me that certain requirements are very important to him. When he started the practice he found that although he was getting results he felt he was holding himself back. He took time to consider why this was and realised it was because, living on the first floor, he was anxious about the possibility of people seeing him. He drew the curtains and immediately had very full spontaneous movement. He explained it was also necessary for him to be alone. What he said referred to him personally, but shows the importance of setting.

To create the right mental setting it is necessary to decide that, for at least half an hour, you have the complete luxury of being able to move and express yourself in any way pleasing you within the physical space you have prepared. What you do within that time doesn't have to make sense. It doesn't have to please anyone else. It does not have to produce anything. It can be quiet, active, noisy, sleepy, aggressive – because there is nobody but yourself involved, nobody to be judged by, and you are going to withhold judgement of yourself until the end of the session.

During the half hour any spontaneous movements that occur might come in waves of activity followed by waves of quietness. If there is quietness, simply rest, holding the 'piano key' feeling in the body so that it is ready to respond to any arising impulses. You do not have to be continually active. Give yourself this period of time in which you allow yourself this liberation. It means letting your being find its own way of resting, its own level of activity, its own path of healing and growth.

In speaking, you seldom know beforehand the words you are going to use, except in a formal situation, but you do have a 'felt sense' of what you are going to say. This only becomes real to you when you actually speak. Likewise, if you think of two friends, you will notice a feeling sense of how different each one is. You have these feeling responses regarding everybody you meet, everything you see. They underlie your whole life, but you may fail to notice them. It is this feeling sense you are going to use and exercise in the next form of movement.

> With all our technology and scientific understanding we cannot create anything near the complexity and wonder of a living creature or a simple life form. Despite this, few modern human beings have much veneration for the process of life as it shows itself in their own bodies. There is certainly a growing attempt to work with the natural, but nearly always with readily-formed techniques. As individuals we also frequently cut ourselves off from what is natural or instinctive in us, perhaps even *because of* our ideals of spirituality or environmental harmony. It is rare to find someone who will lay aside their preconceptions and listen to what their own being has to say. Such listening and learning is real respect. It is an admission that the process of life sustaining us, in its experience of millions of years, in its creative struggle, its countless lives and deaths, has something of great value to show us. It is also an expression of trust that the unconscious secrets of life's experience are communicable to our listening consciousness.

Your Body Is A Moving Sea – Steps In Liberation

You will need about an hour to complete this session. The aim of 'moving sea' is to continue the development of body awareness and spontaneous movement. Once you have used the approach suggested below, there is no need to go through the preparatory stages in future. For instance, do not do the yawning and arm lifting. Go straight into exploring the water movements. These can be used over and over with enjoyment and gain.

1 To start *Phase Two*, repeat any three of the warm-up movements.

2 Remind yourself of the feeling of spontaneous movement by using the 'arm against the wall' exercise.

3 Extend your awareness of how your body and feelings move

spontaneously by simulating yawns and allowing them to develop into stretches or movements.

4 Stand in the middle of your space and close your eyes. Lift your arms from your sides and take your hands high above your head. Do this a few times, noticing the difference in feeling with hands high or low.

5 Pause with hands by your sides. Now hold the *idea* of taking the hands up high again without consciously attempting the movement. Take your time, and be aware of how your hands and arms *want* to make the movement. This means watching to see if the sort of feelings that entered into your yawning and arm exercises are in operation here. If this includes the rest of your body, or if your arms go in a direction other than above your head, that is fine.

6 Stand in your space with eyes closed. Drop unnecessary tensions as you listen to the music. Hold in mind for a moment the idea that you are giving your body space to explore without judgement. Then take the idea of water and let your body explore the expression of the quality of water. There is no need to think up what to do. Let your body explore. Trust it to find its own way to expressive movements. Allow yourself about 30 minutes for this.

7 Let your experience of yawning and listening to how your arms wanted to move be used here. Take time to observe and allow the delicate motivations – magnetic pulls – directing your body to watery movement.

8 You will find you have resources of imagination you did not suspect. Aspects of water you hadn't consciously set out to explore will be expressed in your movements. If you are expressing deep still waters, you will actually feel a deep quietness and power. Or if it is the power of rushing rivers, then a feeling of power will surge through your body as you touch your resources of strength and healing. The flowing feelings that arise are actually healing.

As you learn to trust this process and allow it to grow in expression, you will find that unexpected themes arise. Even though you are expressing water, your expression will have in it feelings that are particular to yourself.

While recently leading a group practising inner-directed movement, I was struck again by how creative we all are if given the right environment. One woman in the group, exhausted from the demands of her job, experienced deep relaxation out of which enthusiasm and pleasurable energy arose, leading her to dance and bathe in her own joy. A man explored his relationship with love, and saw that he needed to gather to himself the love he received from others to call out his own resources of affection. A woman who worked as a nurse met the painful emotions arising from observing the difficulties of a mentally-retarded patient. Her creative movements led her to find a way of accepting the reality of life's difficulties. The pain cleared and she felt she was ready to give a more flowing response to others in difficulty.

You too will find that your creative movements deal with and heal personal situations. I believe this is because the self-regulating or problem-solving process that underlies dreams surfaces during inner-directed movement.

Using the 'water movements' has the benefit of toning the body. It brings harmony between emotions and body. Your feelings are allowed to be active and thereby move towards emotional well-being. Areas of your body and mind not usually allowed pleasure are bathed in it.

Chapter Three

MOVEMENT TO WHOLENESS

LIBERATING THE BODY – PHASE THREE

DISCOVERING YOUR POWER OF GROWTH

Although another approach to inner-directed movement will be described below, I am not suggesting that you avoid using the previous exercises. Using the water movements or yawning, even after dozens of repetitions, will still bring new facets and freshness. Each approach does produce slightly different results, however. The yawning method of starting, for instance, appears to lead more to release of physical tension – the water method leads more to expression of feelings. It is no exaggeration to say that the next method, if used a number of times, helps you to fuller self-expression. It brings to the surface qualities and energy that may have been sleeping in you.

To make this clear, it is easy to see that an acorn has within itself the potential of a full-grown oak tree. Even if the acorn is planted and the emerging tree is a metre high, you can still feel there is a lot more in store. As a human being, even though you are physically mature, there may still be a great deal more of yourself which has not yet become realised externally.

The Seed

Create your environment again, with sufficient space and suitable clothing. This time you will need to play your music quite softly. Again it should be music that does not distract the attention too much. Warm up with two or three of the movements already described. Give yourself up to three-quarters of an hour for the whole session.

The important thing about the 'seed' practice is that you are purposely not imagining a *specific movement* for your body to follow. You are only holding an idea, an outline, and to follow it your body

and feelings must move into the unknown and play creatively with
the idea of the seed to produce any result. So let your body feel its
way slowly into finding its posture or movement. Don't get frustrated
if, in this first practice, little happens. Remember that inner-directed
movement is an acquired skill, and you are still learning.

Not only is this an exercise for your feeling sense, but it is also a
way for the process of inner-directed movement to express itself. You
can consider it a success if some aspect of what arises is spontaneous
or unexpected, so at first it doesn't matter if the session feels
mechanical and contrived. Having those feelings means you are
sensing what is happening and you can thereby refine your technique
with their help.

1 Stand in the centre of your space and raise your arms above your
head. Hold them so they are quite extended.

2 With eyes closed, bring to mind the idea or image of an unplanted
seed. It can be any sort of seed.

3 Notice whether your body in its present posture feels as if it is
expressing the form and condition of the seed. The aim is to
consider how you and your body feel in relationship to the idea
and sense you have of the seed. Many people find, for instance, that
having the arms extended does not 'feel' like an unplanted seed.
Don't struggle with this. It is just an experiment, play with it, have
fun.

4 If you do not notice such feelings of difference between your
extended posture and the idea of a seed, try another approach.
Remember the experiment in which, after raising your arms above
your head several times, you let your arms find their own way to
move. Play with the feelings of what it would be like to have the
shape of the seed; to be waiting for the right conditions to grow
and express all your hidden potential of leaves and flowers. Let your
body play with these ideas or feelings, just as you let it move when
you allowed your arms to find their way upwards. Do not make
this an intellectual inquiry. Use your body and feelings, even if this
is new for you. Explore in this way until you feel you have found
a position that is satisfying. Take your time. Notice whether the
arms and head are right. Would a seed that is not growing feel alert,

sleeping, or waiting? See if you can find an inner mood which for you feels like a seed. Do not attempt to think the whole thing out or consider it scientifically. Let whatever feeling sense you have guide you.

5 When you find a position and inner feeling that suit you, take the next step by letting yourself explore, with body movements, postures and awareness of your feelings, what might happen when you as the seed are planted in warm moist soil and begin to grow. Continue your feeling exploration to find what will occur when you grow, put out leaves, blossoms and fulfil your cycle. Explore the whole cycle of the seed's expression. Don't hold a rigid idea of what the growth of the seed means. The aim is to explore your own feeling sense in regard to the seed's growth.

6 It might be that as the seed you feel very strongly that you do not want to grow. In this case, remain in the form of the seed until you feel a change and an urge to grow, or until your session time is finished.

7 When you sense that the experience has finished, rest quietly for about five minutes and end the session.

The following quote from a letter I received gives an idea of the wide range of experience which can arise from this exercise. Judith describes her use of this 'seed' approach to inner-directed movement as follows:

> I am a trainee yoga teacher and have been teaching for three years. I have a small class of fourteen students who are keen and attend regularly. I decided to have my students try the seed approach to see how they would react. I explained it as well as I could, and the feedback I got was as follows: A man in his thirties said, 'I felt I was in a womb. It was very comfortable, cosy and dark. I wanted to stay there. I didn't want to come away – it was so peaceful. I have never experienced anything like it before'. He was very impressed.
>
> A woman in her thirties felt like throwing her arms around and kicking her legs. 'I felt I wanted to give birth and was about to deliver'. She didn't fling herself about, but held back. I think it was a pity she didn't let go. Perhaps I didn't explain the whole procedure clearly

enough for them to understand that it was entirely free movements. The majority acted out being flowers. Only one in the class thought it was a lot of 'bloody rubbish', her words. She didn't even try. She thought she would feel stupid acting out a seed.

I was surprised at the outcome, that so much should happen first time. I personally felt as if I became the bud of a crocus. I seemed to be slowly unfolding with difficulty. Not until I fully opened did I feel a great relief. The results of this have made me feel very positive in my outlook, and far happier.

Experiencing your growth as the seed is enjoyable without any concern about what it might do or be beneficial for. Its possibilities are worth understanding though. Judith's experience of feeling difficulty in opening, and great relief when opened, typifies its action.

What this means is made clear by the experience of Graham, with whom I worked personally. He found that while being the seed he had no urge whatsoever to grow. He lay on the ground for the whole period and felt how wonderful it was that he didn't have to actively express himself.

When we talked this over Graham told me he could easily see the connection this had with his life. He said that although he was energetic, and as a male nurse had to deal actively with people all day, he never felt he was really present as himself. As a person he hid behind his role as a nurse and seldom exposed his real feelings to other people. In fact he wondered if he had ever really expressed in activity what he felt or believed.

Graham then used the seed approach again. This time he felt the urge to grow and emerge from his non-expression. He gradually opened out from a curled-up position and slowly moved, with hesitations, to a kneeling position. At that point he stopped. He explained that standing up – being present with his own feelings and potential with other people – was so new to him, that the half-way position was as far as he could grow at that time. Nevertheless, it gave him an exultant feeling to be at last, for what he felt as the first time in his life, daring to go into the world as a real human being. He felt sure that in following sessions of the seed approach he would progressively emerge more fully.

The seed approach deals specifically with your growth as a person. It helps you to work out, through creative movement, any restriction in expressing your potential and your physical energy. People who have not lived out their own inner needs, or are unexpressive physically, will find this helpful.

THE SEED GROUP

Part of the pleasure of inner-directed movement is sharing it with others. I still enjoy seeing the pleasure in people who have used inner-directed movement for the first time. Because it is a pleasure, and because sharing provides support and a more powerful atmosphere or 'space', it is worth considering whether a friend or friends would join with you.

The seed approach can also be used with others. If so, one person is the seed, and the supporting people – two to three at the most – can be earth and water. The aim is to support the growth of whoever is the seed by physical and emotional contact.

If you want to use this, the seed starts by standing in the middle of the others, who take time to make contact with her/him. They allow time to find an attitude which enables them to get closer physically and emotionally than in usual social roles. Without forcing or acting mechanically, the members touch and draw near to the seed. When this is established the seed curls up on a prepared space – with blanket or cushions – on the floor. The members draw near and make contact again, getting close, covering the seed's body with their own, penetrating with touch, as does earth and water.

LIBERATING THE BODY – PHASE FOUR

The approaches to inner-directed movement described in the first three phases, although different, all revolve around allowing spontaneous movement. Through the use of these varied approaches you will gain direct experience of your own creativity in working with your body and discovering its links with your language of posture, gesture and movement. You begin to discover the emergence also of spontaneous creative fantasy. It is creative because each of the approaches allows expression of something slightly different – and each session is itself unique in some way.

The next approach is the cornerstone of inner-directed movement. It is presented as the fourth because the other approaches will have made you more practised in the technique. This enables you now to use the great simplicity of the 'open' approach. With the previous approaches there was either a physical activity or theme which gave direction for the practice. These structures are absent in the next approach.

The Open Approach

Most of the great traditional approaches, such as Shaktipat, Seitai, Qi Gong or Subud use this open approach, though they each explain it differently. Its special quality is that it reduces limitations. The other approaches, because they have more structure, direct what arises for you in some measure. It is like walking into a library and saying, 'I am looking for some information on health', or 'I am looking for something about personal growth'. That would limit your search. If you walk into the library and think, 'I am open to discovering anything relevant to my life', then the limitations are fewer.

The open approach is an access to your whole self. Because much of yourself is still unknown to you it is impossible to know just where to look to find your own wholeness and health. You are unique. You have a different background in family or cultural traditions to many others. You have personal and particular life experiences and different personal qualities of mind and body which make your needs distinctive. Allowing your being freedom of expression during inner-directed movement empowers your ability to work at and express your own special needs.

Despite the fact that virtually all the healing or helping professions or techniques attempt to *apply* cures or methods to our being, it is obvious that we know our own needs and are largely self-righting or self-regulating. This is meant in the most down to earth and observable manner. Expressed in its simplest form, if you are hungry you have an urge to eat. Beliefs or fears may degrade that pure urge into other forms. Worries about weight gain; ideas about what is healthy food; habits perverted by trying to be 'one of the boys/girls', may achieve this degrading process.

By opening to inner-directed movement without structure you allow your being to gradually shed such degradations and return to an expression and recognition of your real needs. Because you are always feeling your own personal needs – as in the example of hunger – the open approach to inner-directed movement helps in dropping preconceived ideas and social pressures. There may even be a process of clearing out the habits, fears and pains that have stood in the way of your own healthy self. Then comes the experience of meeting and accepting the real you. The you that is both ordinary and extraordinary.

The adventure of truly integrating the culture you have taken in and forming it into your own personal and living self takes time. It is not going to happen in just four or five sessions of inner-directed movement. But if used for an hour once or twice a week for a year, very real changes will be seen.

Movement Toward Wholeness

Although use of the voice was mentioned, and exercises given in *Phase One*, it is worth remembering the healing value of this. Your voice, your body and your emotions are linked. Restraint in one restrains the others, so working with the voice can help free and mobilise the body and emotions. Tense or rigid emotions are just as difficult to live with as a tense and rigid body. Just as physical pain and restriction arise from muscular tension, emotional pain and limitation derive from emotional blocks.

If there are changes in pace during the period of practice, allow them. The range of possible movements and forms of expression are so enormous it would be boring to list them. They include all tones of feeling from angry to loving and exalted; all vocal expressions from deep crying to imitation of the sound and feeling of foreign languages; all types of movement from the most exquisite stillness to frantic tribal dancing. These are only part of the spectrum of inner qualities you are healthily capable of as a whole human being. Sometimes people say 'I have never expressed myself like this before, I wonder if I am bizarre'. The answer is that only whole human beings are capable of a wide range of expressions which they can choose to end at any moment. It is the unhealthy person who is locked into compulsive and limited patterns of behaviour. Liberation of the body is a sign of health.

1 Prepare your environment.

2 Put on some music which has energy but does not grab your attention too much. Use a couple of warm-up movements to get your circulation more active and your body loosened.

3 Stand in the middle of your space with feet about shoulder width apart. For a few moments hold the thought and feeling that for the next half hour you are giving up your own conscious efforts. You are allowing your being to express its own needs in its own way by opening to the WHOLE you.

4 Get the 'keyboard' feeling in yourself. In other words, give yourself permission to allow spontaneous or unexpected movements of body and mind – don't forget to leave yourself open to vocal expression too.

5 Allow spontaneous movements to develop. Take an open, observing state of mind.

6 If movements are tardy in emerging, start by slowly circling the arms. Make the circles cross in front of the body, both in the pelvis area and above your head.

7 When your arms are moving with ease, become aware of the shapes your fingertips are carving in space. Stay with this observation for a few moments, then notice whether your hands and fingers have any urge to create their own shapes in space. It may feel as if delicate magnetic pulls are directing your hands. If so, follow these delicate urges by letting your arms be moved by them. Let your hands and arms discover any movements or speed which satisfies you. Permit your whole body and voice to become involved if there is a tendency toward this.

8 When you are ready to finish the session, stop the movements and relax on the floor or in an easy chair for a few minutes. There is often a natural sense of an end of the theme that has arisen.

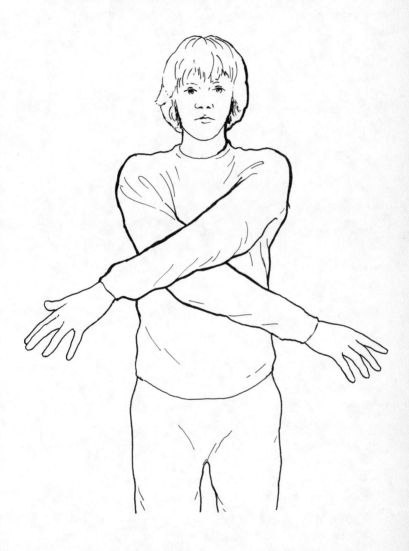

Using the open approach you will experience movements, themes, emotional expression and insights particular to your personal bodily, mental and spiritual needs. The more fully you express the more you learn to command the whole of your being. Liberating the body is movement to wholeness.

Chapter Four

APPROACHES TO LIBERATION

When you have used inner-directed movement to the point where you begin to feel your body and mind are mobile and fluid in it, many avenues for expansion open for you. Details of how to use these different approaches will now be explained. They are all purely supplemental to what has already been described in the earlier chapters. They are given not because they are necessary to do – *the simplest, 'open approach' is the core of the whole practice* – but in case you want to explore the possibilities of this new skill.

SEITAI AND THE HEALING TOUCH

Noguchi taught three approaches to the Japanese form of inner-directed movement which he named Seitai. The first approach, katsugen-undo, is basically the same as what I have described as the open approach. My observation of it is that the only difference is that the voice is not allowed so much freedom in Japan. In fact each approach produces slightly different results, due most likely to the cultural attitudes, group expectations and environment present in each system.

There are three given movement/postures preceding katsugen-undo. In Japan these are performed from the position of sitting on one's heels. If this is difficult, however, try them either from a kneeling position, or kneeling, then sitting back onto a thick cushion or books. The movements are devised to produce a mixture of relaxation and tension after which one will have a desire to stretch and move.

Posture One

1 From the position of kneeling and sitting back on your heels, or
   onto books or a cushion to take your weight off your heels, place

your fingertips on your upper abdomen, just above your navel. The aim is to be aware of whether you are tensing your abdomen and to keep it relaxed during the movement.

2 Take a slow breath in, and as you do so imagine you are filling your being not only with fresh air, but also with light and health. As much as possible, feel the positive force of cleansing fill your body.

3 As you slowly breathe out let your trunk drop forward towards the floor, feeling relaxed and keeping the abdomen free of tension. Also, imagine you are breathing out all darkness and ill health from your being.

4 As you inhale bring your trunk to the upright position again, once more imagining breathing in light and health. Continue this movement and breathing meditation until you feel satisfied with it and more relaxed. If there is any desire to yawn during these movements, allow it. This is much encouraged in Seitai.

Posture Two

1 The aim of this movement is to produce tension in the body. From the sitting position breathe in fairly quickly and lift your hips no more than three inches from your heels. As you do this twist your trunk and arms to the left.

2 Hold that tense position for a few moments then drop back into the sitting position with a quick out-breath.

3 Repeat this turning to the right, and continue twisting to alternate sides until you feel satisfied with the movement.

4 End by turning one last time to the right, to balance your starting turn.

Posture Three

1 This is the last of the preliminary posture/movements. This should only be performed three times, at the end of which you should relax and allow your body to stretch or move in any way it wishes.

Allow these free movements to continue for about twenty minutes or longer if you are inclined.

2 Place your thumbs across your palms towards your little fingers. Clasp your fingers around your thumbs tightly to form a fist.

3 Bend your arms at the elbows so that your hands and upper arms are vertical, and your lower arms are horizontal. Breathe in and pull your head and arms back slightly to create a tension between the shoulders and at the base of the neck.

4 Hold the tension for a few seconds then breathe out in a gasp and relax your arms. Do this three times and allow spontaneous movement.

Teachers of Seitai place a lot of stress upon relying on your own being's internal healing functions. In the book *Colds And Their Benefits* Noguchi points out that people who are ill have often lost sensitivity to their body's natural response. As examples he says that such people, on trying to relax, actually tense their body. They are unaware of their natural feelings of tiredness, perhaps they bury them with artificial stimulants such as coffee. Their body does not expand and contract naturally, but is stiff and immobile. Their own healing processes have been denied again and again. The cure for this is to start allowing spontaneous action again. Symptoms of illness must not be suppressed by drugs. Such symptoms are signs of the body trying to heal itself, so must be worked with rather than against. The aim is not to cure the symptom, such as a headache, but to heal the causes. Noguchi goes so far as to say that really healthy people always have slight feelings of illness because they are aware of their reactions to the environment, and are constantly adjusting to it.

Noguchi stresses that it is not the movements of Seitai which heal us. To do the movements mechanically as if they were the cure itself is to miss the whole point and be a return to the strictures of keep-fit. But once you have learnt to allow your body to heal itself more vigorously, you do not need to practise. It is cooperating with the process of your being's own regulating and growth forces that is important. As you gain experience of this it becomes natural and automatic in your everyday life, so doesn't need 'practice'. Noguchi defines the use of Seitai as a movement to train the autonomic nervous system: if your body's capacity to order itself becomes sensitive, your body will naturally maintain itself in a normal, pleasurable condition. This could be compared to an experienced windsurfer who is much more sensitive to the movements of the board than a novice. The experienced windsurfer is always moving into balance, and has much finer adjustments, while the novice can only function on an awkward and very basic level.

Noguchi teaches that an open and receptive state of mind is needed, and this he calls 'tenshin'. Anybody who has watched a cat in motion can see that occasionally it will instinctively do certain stretches or movements. Babies have this open state of mind also, and they can be seen to make a great many movements and sounds spontaneously. Therefore, if you have a relaxed state of mind in which your body is allowed free expression, katsugen-undo will occur by itself. Maybe you will start to stretch, yawn, or even scratch without thinking about it or directing the process.

For those who are so out of balance they are not aware of their body's needs, initial help from another practitioner is useful. To this end Seitai has an approach named yuki – pronounced rather like you-key. It means to touch.

YUKI – TOUCH HEALING – TOUCH PLAY

In the Far East there is a concept concerning human energy or life force which is known as ki. In China it is called chi, as in Tai Chi. Noguchi describes ki as the force behind the formation of the body and its processes. He says it is the ki that directs cellular processes and causes them to grow in the correct shape and size to form our human body. Our movements come from within, directed by ki. In its expression, ki is felt as our motivations. These motivations may cause us to move an arm or a leg. But more important still, without motivations, as can be seen in some people who retire and lose their motivation, every being loses its health. Therefore, Noguchi says that instead of treating the shell, the body, one ought in such cases to treat the ki and to restore the quality of its positive motivations.

Most ancient cultures have developed explanations of this subtle energy field within and around the body. Western science and medicine is now beginning to be able to demonstrate it also. Dr Dolores Krieger, a professor of nursing at New York University, became interested in the subject after studying the work of Oscar Esteban, a Hungarian healer. After studying with Dora Kunz, Krieger was able to work with the energy field in effective healing. She went on to teach 'therapeutic touch' to nurses in a master's level course at New York University.

Valerie Hunt, a professor of kinesiology at UCLA, has been able to demonstrate the presence and importance of the energy field using an electromyograph, a device which measures electrical activity in the muscles.

The Japanese teach that when you place your hands on another person's body, you respond to it. You will feel the energy field if you take time to watch your sensations with awareness. Sometimes your hands feel cold, or there is the sensation of ants crawling on them. If there is a cold response, it may be that there is a lack of vitality in that part of their body. You must continue yuki – that is, directing ki energy – until the hands return to normal. They also say that you will gradually learn to work with these subtle feelings with greater discernment through practice. Noguchi says that on the part of the person receiving yuki there are observable changes. Their pulse rate increases, they feel more relaxed and sometimes sleepy. The effects are 1) relaxation, 2) heightened sensitivity, and 3) discharge. Yuki is certainly of great help, and at present there is much research into how such techniques can be used in healing the sick.

The way I was taught yuki was very simple and without any theoretical background. It is as follows:

The Practice Of Yuki

Yuki is practised with two people. There can of course be many couples using yuki at the same time. One person is the receiver and one the giver. The Japanese who taught me did not limit themselves with ideas of the healthy healing the sick. They used yuki because it was fun to do. But it can be used to help someone who is below par.

1 The receiver can choose whether to lie down, sit or stand, and should become quiet and receptive to the giver. The giver allows

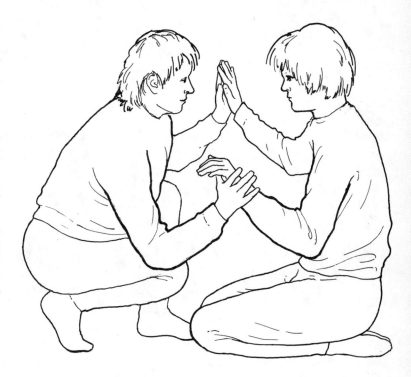

their own inner-directed movements, as occurs in katsugen-undo. But the giver holds in mind that what they are allowing is in response to the receiver. I have found that a useful way to begin is to be about three feet away from the receiver and hold your hands out towards them as if warming your hands. From there follow the delicate urges to move. The idea is not to massage the person, but touch is allowed as you simply follow what your hands and body want to do.

2 The receiver can also allow their own movements in response to the contact with the giver. In watching the Japanese use yuki, there were all levels of response. Sometimes the receiver remains very quiet, even sleepy. Other times both partners move into a lovely dance of responsive spontaneous movement and contact – or a

fast moving play with lots of laughter. The contact may be delicate or full. Very often the hands of the giver do not touch the receiver, but move at a distance from them.

3 The receiver is to be respected. In Western groups who were unfamiliar with 'tenshin' or waiting, on occasion I have seen the giver drop any openness to the needs of the receiver and consciously decide what ought to happen, and drag a receiver to their feet. The giver felt that was where they ought to go. The inner situation or movements of the receiver were thus completely ignored. This non-respect for another person's integrity is not the way to use yuki. The interaction between giver and receiver in yuki, if allowed to develop naturally, often shifts to a mutual giving and receiving.

The experience of yuki is one of the most delightful facets of inner-directed movement. Not only does it develop sensitivity in a relationship, it also enables two people to discover a world of non-verbal communication and meeting. It develops the sensitivity of responsiveness necessary in intimate relationships. Finding that the Japanese had developed this gentle way of strangers meeting and touching showed me an unsuspected side to their culture. In the West, people have sincerely thanked me for showing them how to discover their own beauty and flow in meeting another person.

Working With a Sick Person

The Japanese practitioners of Seitai say that yuki can be useful if a person is feeling unwell. If the person you are giving yuki to is actually ill, there need be no change in the way you give it. It is best if you have practised inner-directed movement for some time to feel easy with allowing spontaneous movement. It is enough to hold the sick person in mind and open yourself to what arises from within. It doesn't even matter if physical contact is not made.

In Subud, the movements (latihan) are sometimes allowed in the presence of a sick person. Unlike yuki, there is no attempt to touch the sick person. Members of Subud are not allowed to work with the opposite sex when giving healing or help with questions. This must be understood as being a culturally created difference. It is important to remember, however, that the different approaches demonstrate the significant fact that the process can work well in various settings and ways. The physical distance of thousands of miles in reality makes no difference. The biggest barrier is not distance or even the degree of illness, it is the beliefs, convictions and limitations we live within.

Open to your inner-directed movements keeping in mind the person who needs support. It does not matter whether the person is near to you or many miles away.

PATHS OF WONDER AND JOY

The dimensions of experience you can meet within yourself through inner-directed movement appear to be without limits. If you have tried the different approaches described above and in the earlier chapters, you will have seen that a slight shift of attitude or a different image or question held in mind focuses you in another experience. This means that as long as you have established yourself in the basic open and surrendered process, you can reach into many different areas of your own potential.

The pathways described below are not absolutely necessary in practising inner-directed movement. It may be, however, that you get special help from using these pathways, even though the simplest form of the practice – the 'open approach' – is the most profound, because you are unique and have your own special needs. Opening your being to allowing spontaneous movement is still the basis of each pathway.

The pathways do have great powers of healing and personal growth. This is because you are not just a physical body. As I have already stated, your internal nature can become stiff and aching through lack of activity, just as your body does. The pathways are designed to take you through a series of experiences that mobilise your being in a way which is only possible if you lead an extraordinarily full and wide life. If you work through these pathways you will emerge feeling a very different person, and in real ways reborn. To get to this point it is not enough to practise each path once. You will need to use each one until you feel easy and fluid in it. If you are using the first one, 'Contraction and Expansion', being easy and fluid means that you can move easily between the opposites, and any tensions or hesitations within the practice have been worked through. This does not mean you have to stick with one path to the exclusion of the others until it is perfect. By all means move around in them to add variety.

> The pathways are great sources of healing and personal growth. They will bring about a remarkable change in your experience of life and relationships. They will open doors to aspects of your own talents and love not previously met. They will take you into an awareness of what was previously invisible within you.

Contraction And Expansion

This is similar to the 'seed approach'. The only difference is that instead of taking the idea of a seed and allowing your being to explore it spontaneously, you first take the idea of contraction, then the idea of expansion.

This is to do with fundamental life processes. If you watch your chest for a while you will observe its contractions and expansions in breathing. Your heart too constantly contracts and expands. Sleeping and waking contract and expand consciousness. Life and death are an expansion and contraction. Perhaps even the universe goes through such a cycle.

1 Create and stand in your space – with or without music.

2 Observe for a minute or so the contraction and expansion of your chest. As you do so allow the feeling of letting yourself drop more fully into the contraction and emptiness. Contraction might also be defined as giving up, feeling empty of any urge to do anything, dropping out of social activity. Allow your body to find its own spontaneous expression of this in posture, movement, and even sound if there is an urge to do so.

3 If you find it difficult to find a spontaneous posture of contraction, try kneeling on the floor and going down into a heap or curling up in a ball. This is a position of contraction.

4 As you go into your expression of contraction hold in mind that you will wait in the contraction to see if any urge towards expansion

occurs. This may take time, or not happen at all, so be willing to wait.

5 Explore how your body as a whole contracts. What does this mean as far as a posture or movement is concerned? What does it feel like inside? What does it mean in your life?

6 If movements and feelings arise leading to expansion, go along with them. Just observe and let yourself take in what arises.

7 If there are conflicts or painful memories holding you in one of the attitudes – contraction or expansion – these will be discharged during the practice.

> Using the pathway of expansion and contraction heals any area of your being locked in one or other of these opposites. The practice enables you to learn to move easily in and out of these opposites that play such a big part in life. If you are stuck in an expansionary attitude, then the practice will balance you – or vice versa.

I Am

This is a very simple way of encouraging the flow of self-expression. Although simple it can be very satisfying and interesting to do. You will need plenty of space for this – enough room to pace about without feeling restricted. Comfortable clothes are also important. The length of time can be anything from ten minutes at the minimum to half an hour, depending on how absorbed you become in what arises.

1 Start by walking around your space. Aim to get an easy flowing pace without having to worry about where you are walking or having to change direction.

2 When you feel easy and relaxed in your pacing, start repeating the words 'I am'. Keep repeating this as you pace and allow yourself to complete the sentence in any way that occurs. So you might simply keep on saying 'I am', but the feeling might change. Or you might say, 'I am bored of this', 'I am feeling frustrated', 'I am always getting myself into arguments' or 'I am so happy'. Whatever comes

to mind, whatever arises spontaneously, allow it to flow through into words and the pacing. This will probably mean that what you say and feel will change as time passes.

3 It is important to have something of the 'piano key' open feeling in yourself as you use this approach. Let whatever ridiculous, beautiful, painful or meaningful feelings about yourself during the practice be stated as fully as you can in the pacing and the 'I am' statements.

The I Am approach leads to a fuller realisation of who you are. It aids in easy self-expression, and is enjoyable and interesting to do.

African Dancing

This might better be called 'native dancing'. But the name is used because most of us have seen film of African villagers or tribespeople celebrating a dance. The movements are often very repetitive and powerful. The use of stamping is frequently used to beat out a rhythm. Movements of the pelvis are often a part of it. There is open expression of all the basic drives, from sex to awe of the divine. Suppression of our own earthy and divine feelings may lead to tension and depression. The use of African dancing is very invigorating and helpful in being more happily assertive or expressive.

The following description of African dance appeared in the magazine *Mothering*, Winter 1990, under the title *African Dance and Childbirth*. It was written by Amy Trussell.

In Black Africa, many women traditionally pride themselves on being dancers and birthers – endeavors that require uncompromising physical strength, mental clarity, rhythmic integrity, and a direct link to forces greater than themselves. As dancers they give birth, bringing to the birth process the tremendous strength acquired over years of night-long – and sometimes week-long – 'spirit dances'. Daily work, the honoring of womanhood, the deities, the ancestors, the darkness, and the celebration of birth itself are all depicted in the dance. And the dance is carried into the fibers of everyday life.

1 There is no need to *learn* African dancing. Deep within us we all remember our ancient heritage. We are all descendants from our African ancestors, from our primeval forebears who danced. To start you may need a recording of native drumming, but even this is not essential. If you use a recording, stand in your space and let your body feel the drum beats.

2 Do not attempt to take control of your body to follow the sounds. Let your body find its own movement and its own theme to dance. If you stumble and get out of time, don't let this stop you. This is not a dance competition. You are not trying to win a cup.

3 Let your feet, your body, your emotions and voice move with the drums. Allow your strength, your womanhood or manhood, to flow into the movements with exuberance. Be aware of the movement of your breasts, pelvis and genitals, and let pleasure flow from them.

4 If you wish, when you have used African dance a few times, dance out some big event in your life, like the death of a close friend or relative, if such things have happened. Dance marriage, dance the struggle and wonder of growing up, dance your life!

African dance puts you in touch with the roots of life – with being a man or woman in the body – with the power of emotions and love, of loss and gain – with the courage to feel the joy and pain of life. Through it you reclaim the so-called primitive in you that links you with nature and the fundamental life drives. Through it the events of your individual life, its pains and joys, are allowed to connect with a greater whole that sustains you.

The Animal

This approach is quite playful and enjoyable. It could introduce you to movements and feelings you were not in touch with before.

To meet the animal in you is not only to contact the part of yourself stuck in fixed repertoires of response to people and situations. Such fixed responses – which might be as simple as only saying 'Good morning' to the people you meet in the street and never getting beyond that to deeper friendship – trap you. They are habits of behaviour that need reorganisation. But there is also the wonderful wisdom of your internal animal as well, with its deep understanding of relationships and body language. The meeting with your 'animal' can therefore be multi-faceted. It is in mammals that playful behaviour developed and is very marked. Many humans have lost this easy physical contact and playfulness with each other, and this can be regained through meeting your 'animal'.

The experience of your internal animals, or the traits you have gathered through love from animals you have known, may surface during your general practice of inner-directed movement. To touch it directly you can try this path to the animals.

1 After setting up your 'space' drop any arising thoughts as well as you can for about fifteen minutes. During this time hold your attention on your physical sensations and inner feelings.

2 Allow any movements and responses to external noises and environment to arise only from your physical sensations – sight, touch, smell, taste, hearing – and from feelings such as comfort, discomfort, pleasure, pain, restlessness, tiredness, but not from your thinking. Explore your environment from this basic level of yourself – comfort, discomfort and your feelings. Look for a comfortable place like a dog would. Rub against the furniture as if you were a cat. If you are with friends using this path, meet each other without speech, but through smell and physical contact.

3 As you enter into this allow your inner-directed movements to emerge, permitting your inner animal to express itself. Let it lead you along and show you its view of the world and its wisdom or its needs in your life.

4 When you begin to get the feel of this, start with the awareness of physical and feeling responses again while crawling or lying on the floor. From the feelings of an animal, sensitive to sound, feeling its own instinctive aliveness and desire to survive – its survival anxiety – take time to see if you can stand up. See if you can discover what it means to stand up with all your senses and feelings working.

5 Another approach is to start again from basic physical and sensory awareness. Move about in this for a while, then explore what it might have been like for the human animal to become self-conscious, to discover its own body, to look at itself in water or a mirror with a sense of 'I'.

Giving permission for the animal within you to emerge enlarges your experience of yourself and the world. It can help heal the hurts and reactive fears felt by this aspect of yourself because it is the animal that senses fear. Passion for life can be regained, for it is the animal that feels honest and strong feelings about life. Your body can regain its natural pride and pleasure in movement, and the war between the intellect and the basic drives can be resolved. Through it you can gain new levels of perception of other people and society, and even find new abilities.

Being Born

In Seitai there is no exploration of the mental and emotional possibilities of the practice. For many people inner-directed movement is largely an enjoyment of their body's activity with some accompanying shift of feelings as the movements are enjoyed. In fact, there is no need to explore deeply the realms of the psyche to gain great enjoyment and benefits from its use. However, I would not be properly describing what is achievable through the technique if I did not give a small introduction to what might be found within the enormous realms of your mind and memory. The approaches given below are therefore for those who wish to open the door to an exploration of their own interior world of experience.

There is, however, a warning which needs to be sounded here. The experience of your own inner life is very real. It may put you in contact with areas of yourself which you may not have met before as an adult. Therefore, unless you already have experience of working therapeutically – as with psychotherapy – it is best only to use this aspect of inner-directed movement with a supportive group to start with. It is a bit like learning to swim. If you use the approaches below successfully they might introduce you to the deep waters of your feelings. So, like swimming, until you gain confidence in dealing with the new environment, it is best to learn with others. Of course, if you have already worked in this way there is no problem. Or if you are a group leader working therapeutically, the approaches are gentle ways into personal growth.

The following approaches are described for those who wish to explore something of the psychologically therapeutic side of inner-directed movement. If you are content with your experience of the practice as it is, there is no need at all to explore the mental and emotional side of yourself.

Being born is not only an important physical event, but also a truly powerful psychological process. It is a well-documented, although not yet generally accepted fact that unborn babies have memorable experiences, and that birth itself leaves strong memories and influences. Thousands of people have now recovered memories of birth through various forms of therapy, meditation and hypnosis. Some of these areas of experience suggest that consciousness is in some degree continuous throughout all levels of being. (See *The Secret Life of The Unborn Child* by Dr Thomas Verny, MD, and John Kelly – Sphere Books Ltd, UK 1982/Summit Books, USA 1981.)

To take the path of birth in inner-directed movement may mean recovering memories of your own birth and how it influenced your development. Such memories are completely non verbal and are composed purely of physical and emotional experience and body postures and movements. Apart from personal memories, though, you may discover *the power of renewal and the urge to grow expressed in the symbol of birth*. This was described well by Judith, in Chapter 3, when she felt like a crocus flower, struggling to open. In this way you might touch resources within yourself that hold the key to emerging from old and restricting emotions, habits and ways of life.

1 If possible do this with two or three friends who are supportive and used to the action of inner-directed movement. This is not

because it is unsafe, but because with friends you can create an excellent 'womb' environment.

2 If with friends, create your 'space' with enough room for you all to occupy a place close together on a soft duvet or blanket on the floor. Sit together making contact through holding hands, and centre down into the mood of what you are doing. Imagine yourself slipping backwards to the time when you were in the womb. When ready, break contact and take an appropriate position in the middle of the blanket. Try curling up, knees to chest. Your friends should now make close physical contact and cover you with their bodies so you are comfortable but enclosed in the warmth of their physical contact.

3 Relax and wait for inner-directed movements to arise. There is no need to concentrate on the theme of being born. It is enough for you to have thought about this at the beginning. Now you can let go of any thoughts and *wait* and *watch*.

4 Do not attempt to make anything happen, or perform something for your friends. If all you do is to lie there for half an hour without movement, just do that. It is a very rewarding experience just to be quiet and close to friends in this non-verbal way. But you will probably find that after a few minutes there are changes of feeling occurring within you, and waves of impulse leading to some sort of movement or expression of feelings. Let these waves roll through you. Any movements that occur will come in waves too, so drop into quiet resting between them, and let the process unfold.

5 If practising by yourself – or alone in a group – imagine yourself going back in time and size to the point where you are in the womb ready to be born. Take up a position on your blanket that expresses this as nearly as you can. Then allow inner-directed movement as described in 3 and 4 above.

6 What emerges will be unique to yourself, but in general it may feel like a direct experience of your own birth and relationship with your mother. Or it may be felt as an experience of psychological birth – a leaving behind of past attitudes and ways of expressing yourself that you have outgrown. You might realise that for much

of your life you have hardly been alive, and at last you are born and are living.

7 Perhaps what happened was incomplete, and you will need to use the path again to carry it further. Birth is such a major feature, you will need to come back to this theme anyway to really find the treasure of insights and energy dormant in it.

8 Whatever has arisen, it is helpful to write it down and consider if you can see any relevance to your everyday life.

Joe, who used this path in his forties, experienced a difficult birth. He discovered a strong feeling of not wanting to be born, of a desire to avoid life by staying in the womb. His birth had been two months premature, so he could understand the feelings of not being ready to be involved in life. He had always had strong feelings of not wanting to participate in what other people were doing, of wanting to withdraw at social gatherings. On practising the 'birth' pathway again the feeling of withdrawal gradually receded and was replaced by a readiness to be involved in life. This made an observable difference to the way he met other people and was ready to be a part of activities.

If you practised with friends or within a group, share your experience with them and talk over what relevance you feel it might have to your everyday life. Also, ask for their comments on what they felt or observed. It is important to clarify for yourself what habits of feeling or attitude your birth has left, and how you wish to change these.

The Pathway of birth offers the discovery of change in the amount of yourself you can bring to expression in relationship and work. It develops the ability to drop the past and to leave what is outgrown behind. Facets of yourself that were never really alive before can be born and live.

The Baby And Child
One of the tragedies of adult life is that you may have forgotten your childhood. You may still remember events and dates, but the intensity

of feelings, the real insight into the world of childhood may be lost.

Can you remember how it was to live before time began for instance? The sense of time is learnt. Prior to being able to speak, and to your concept of time, you lived in eternity. Days lasted forever. A week was infinite in its multitude of impressions and experience.

Can you remember your first love affair – with your mother? Being your first, its wonder or devastation has coloured all your love since. But if you can't remember then you are living out the wonder or pain without awareness.

Discovering your internal baby and child is to find some of the great secrets of your life. Many of the decisions you make about work or sexual partners have their roots there. What may appear as destiny often starts from deeply felt experiences in your childhood. Who you consider yourself to be is not an immutable reality. Your genetic inheritance gave you a foundation, but what was built upon that was due to the events of your childhood. If you are not entirely satisfied with the results, a lot of DIY alterations can take place.

1   You are going back along the time track of your life. Leaving behind the many things you have collected as you moved into the adult years – bank accounts, bills, mortgage, work, family responsibilities, dependents, car, the 'musts' and 'shoulds' and 'should nots'.

2   Although you can target a particular time of your childhood simply by thinking about it for a few moments, leave it open. Stand in your space, with or without music, and allow whatever movements and emotions arise. Do not be in a hurry. Sometimes it takes quite a time to gradually build the inner change necessary to recreate childhood feeling states. Remember that many years of childhood were without refined language. This means the experiences of that period were wholly physical sensations, movements and emotions. That is not to say you didn't have a mind, but its perceptions were very immediate and not filtered through words and past associations. Give yourself time and opportunity to drop the top layers of yourself and your present habits of experiencing the world.

3   Do not get confused by thinking that you have to *act* like a child to make this a successful experience. What you are doing is to give

yourself time and opportunity to experience your child self on an inner level. So it does not matter that externally you do not act or speak like a child. Use the same approach as the water exploration in the exercise on page 56.

4 The likely response is that you will experience some feelings, some event from childhood, that is important in your life because of its effect. As childhood is such a vulnerable period, it may take time to get to free-flowing feelings on this pathway. The clearing of hurt emotions and attitudes might be necessary first. Nevertheless, this is an extremely worthwhile process.

5 Many of your important habits were formed during your childhood. As an example – if you were an only child and had to spend much time alone, you may have got into the habit of suppressing your desire for company. If this habit persists it comes to be felt as normal. In fact it is neither normal nor abnormal, it is simply the way you have shaped yourself. In adult life you might therefore find it strange or difficult to be with groups of people. If this becomes a nuisance and you want to change, it would be helpful to see this character trait as a habit rather than an immutable part of yourself. If you identify with it as yourself, there will be some resistance to change.

6 It is important to consider what you experience in your childhood pathway in the light of what habits it has formed. Many habits are very supportive, we might then call them skills, such as language.

The baby and childhood pathway allows some of the most permanent and importantly positive life changes to occur through clearing the accumulation of emotional debris built up during early growth. Resistance to positive change often has its roots in this area. This is not only because of 'emotional debris' but some of the most durable and defended habits were put into operation or developed in this period of your growth. The reason we generated these habits was nearly always out of necessity at the time. The habits helped us to survive – THEN – but may be self defeating and undermining today. Once their rationale is seen it becomes easier to change these habits.

BODY DOWSING – RELEASING THE UNCONSCIOUS WISDOM

Every movement we make is an expression of our feelings, of what we think and will to do, of our unconscious emotions and ideas. Very often our movements express habits, such as walking along a road and, without thought, taking the turning for home when we really want to go to the shop. Through movement we show what we may not yet have fully thought or understood. And it is because of this aspect, especially as it arises through spontaneous movement, that such practices as dowsing are possible.

Dowsing, in various forms, has been known throughout history and the world for centuries. In early European history dowsing became associated with a rod or forked stick, and was used to help find water, precious metals in the soil, coal, and lost objects. Despite the scientific scepticism of our times, dowsing is still widely used even by government departments – because it works.

Dowsing is not always connected with a stick or rod. Navaho Indians practise what they call 'trembling hands'. After a simple ritual they allow their hands to move spontaneously. From these movements they understand questions asked of them. The American anthropologist Dr Clyde Kluckhohn and his wife investigated a practitioner on a Navaho reservation. Mrs Kluckhohn had lost her handbag three days previously so asked the practitioner, Gregorio, if he could find it. Standing in the open air on a hill, and after rubbing corn pollen on his hands, Gregorio was able to tell them the location of the handbag. This was later confirmed.

Dr Paul Brunton, in his book *Search In Secret India*, tells of his meeting with an Indian ascetic who used his arms to answer questions. He would allow his arms to move spontaneously, and from their movements could give a yes or no response. Indian dowsers do not use a rod, but experience powerful changes of sensation in their body, and are thus able to detect sources of water and minerals.

While investigating the intuitive faculties of Australian Aborigines, Ronald Rose tells of a more refined form of body dowsing. In his book *Living Magic* (Chatto and Windus, 1957) he says that the tribesmen he lived with used different areas of their body to represent relatives. So their father might be represented by their right forearm, their mother by their left forearm, their first uncle by their right biceps, and so on. In this way, if an unaccountable pain or sensation developed in a part of the body, they were able to tell which relative was hurt or needed help. Rose witnessed this in action and describes it as extremely accurate and reliable.

All of these forms of dowsing, even when a rod is used, depend upon the involuntary responses acting through the body in answer to a question. Taken overall they demonstrate the wide range of ways in which such responses can be sought or experienced. All are ways to call upon the information we have perhaps unknowingly gathered in our unconscious, or upon our intuition. It is now understood that the most fundamental way in which unconscious information or feelings are expressed is through gestures or body movements. The next level of expression for unconscious content is through symbolic behaviour such as mime or drama. Freud demonstrated that slips of the tongue were another way of letting our innermost but inhibited feelings show. This explains how knowledge we cannot yet vocalise clearly can be expressed through such subtle body movements as dowsers experience.

Within the practice of Subud there is a technique which synthesises all these approaches. It is called 'testing'. In testing it is accepted that clear and helpful information can be gained by allowing inner-directed movement to arise in response to a question. Members of Subud often use this method to clarify the suitability of a new member to the practice, or to find what may help a sick member. It can be used to explore any question.

ENHANCING YOUR INTUITION

Dreams and imagination are a multifaceted way of sensing things. If you consider an early human being, prior to the emergence of complex speech and the ability to think in the abstract symbols we call words, all their thoughts would most likely have been in images like a waking dream. A human couple in the dawn of our history, standing in wild terrain and seeing dust on the horizon, would need to know very quickly whether the dust was a sign of food or of an enemy. Without the tool of thought, they would have relied upon their emotional response and their unconscious scanning of experience and instincts to aid them. The result would have been experienced as urges to movement and emotion, and as mental imagery. I believe it is because of this long period in our past history, when our ancestors relied on what we might now call intuition – this rapid scanning of information beneath conscious awareness – that we still have this latent ability of insight without reasoning.

You can reclaim something of these lost abilities through the use of inner-directed movement. The amplification of the intuitive link between your conscious self and your unconscious occurs because body dowsing – I will refer to it as inquiring or inquiry from here on – allows the basic forms of internal communication described above to be operative. Movement, emotions, sound and imagery are all freed to be used as means of expressing unconscious content or intuitive insights.

> The general use of inner-directed movement reopens the door between your conscious self and your unconscious through your intuition. Inquiry enables this connection to be used to access the practical and spiritual resources you need. Inquiry works because it relies on the fundamental ways your conscious self receives information from within.

COMMUNICATING WITH YOUR INNER GUIDE

It is important to reconnect with the best in you, with the mass of unconscious life experience and intuition you hold within, with the shoreless sea of life of which you are a part. It is not like fortune-telling or Ouija boards or a party trick. It is a meeting with the extra stores of wisdom in yourself. But do not think of the information or insight you gain as if it were an oracle or prophecy. You are the creator of your life. You ask for inner help to gain more insight, more information from which to make wise decisions – not to search for something to hand decisions over to.

The possible uses for inquiry are:

Help in understanding life problems
Unravelling the meaning of a dream

Information about illness and what might be done to help
Fresh insights into any research project
Suggestions for creative ideas about work
Finding lost objects
Help in making difficult decisions
Deeper understanding of a person you are dealing with in your work or in your relationships
Insight into your spiritual life and growth.

At first you may be 'stiff' in your response, but even so you will usually get a direct reaction. A more fluid or subtle response – one in which greater detail or insight arises – comes with practice. The following steps are designed to help even the least intuitive of people find greater access to their own wider awareness. If you find your experience of inner-directed movement is very fluid, has full emotional response and leads to insights, these first stages are not necessary. Move on the section on *Advanced Options of Extending Your Awareness*.

First Steps in Extending Your Awareness

Imagine you are going to communicate with a part of yourself that has an unlimited amount of information and influence to share with you. What this dimension of yourself gives you will be in direct response to what you ask. The question you ask will be the factor shaping the response, so it is occasionally worth asking what is the right question to get effective help. Remember that all you receive has to pass through your own body, your emotions and your mind. YOU are the instrument that transforms the communication into understandable experience. If your body is full of tensions and drugs there will obviously be interference. If your emotions are taut with anxiety, flooded with disbelief, there will be blockages. If your mind is rigid in its opinions, locked into habits of thought, you will need to practise listening and receiving. Even if you can be ready to drop these for a few moments the channel can clear.

One of the basic actions of inner-directed movement is to make your body and psyche more mobile. This mobility gradually produces a greater intuitive link with your unconscious, and thus the collective experience and creative impulse of your life.

1 Because the basic level of your intuitive sense tends to express itself as body movements and symbols, it brings a quicker response if you use these from the start, and gradually drop them as your ability refines.

2 Create your 'space' and environment as described in the initial practices. Use background music if it helps.

3 Stand in the middle of your space and do two or three of the warming-up movements.

4 Get into the responsive 'piano key' feeling. Mentally ask how your body will give you a 'no' signal. Each person has a different way of signalling 'no': your signal may be head shaking, or perhaps a particular movement of a hand or some other part of your body.

5 Getting this 'no' response is the first step in a growing communication between your conscious self and your unconscious faculties. Try it a few times until you are clear about the signal. If there is any uncertainty *ask your unconscious for clarification.*

Always remember – every part of you is vitally alive and full of intelligence. Your body and mind will respond and communicate if you can listen.

6 Now ask for the 'yes' response. Your body will move and give another movement to signify a positive response.

7 Although the 'yes' and 'no' responses are very basic, they have enormous uses, and many questions which need clarification can be explored deeply by this type of investigation. After all, the amazing processes of computers are founded on series of 'yes' and 'no' responses. For instance, if you are investigating a health question you could ask whether your diet is okay in general. If there is a 'yes' response, you could ask if a particular aspect of your diet is at fault. Further questions will depend on whether the response is 'yes' or 'no'.

8 When you have practised using this 'yes' and 'no' response, you can enlarge the vocabulary used in the communication. Your unconscious will readily accept or even suggest symbols or symbolic movement. This means you could set up a sort of 'keyboard' representing aspects of the question you want to pursue.

I watched a very capable and impressive dowser at work, and was struck by the excellent system he had for communicating with his unconscious source of information. He found water by allowing a series of movements with his wand, so that the movements and their strength were the symbols he worked with. Once he had found the site, however, he tested for depth. He did this by simply calling out a depth and watching the reaction. He would say, for example, '20 feet – 30 feet – 40 feet' until the agreed reaction occurred.

This is rather like the 'yes'/'no' reaction already dealt with, but it has a difference. The reaction has already been agreed, so he does not have to go through a lot of 'yes'/'no' questions.

9 I have found some useful ways of putting this into practice. You can create a visual or imaginary symbolic map on the floor. A very elementary one would be a straight line. If you stood on the straight line stretching to your right and left, the area behind you could represent the past or your inner world, and the area ahead of you, the future or the external world. Your movements in relationship to this line would describe what area of experience – past/future, inner/outer – you were exploring.

10 Symbolic movements such as turning to face backwards or reaching forwards could equally well be used to represent these same concepts. Or you can ask what body movements represent the various aspects of the question you are exploring. Thus, if you were exploring a business question and calling on your innate experience and intuition to look at a problem, you could create a map of the different areas such as manufacture, finance, work force, etc. Or you could ask what movements represented these before you started.

Although this may sound clumsy, and it certainly is less streamlined than the more accomplished ways of enhancing insight, it is amazing how much information can be gained in this way with practice. Also, for people who think they completely lack the intuitive faculty, these stages are ways to make accessible what appeared unobtainable.

Advanced Options of Extending Your Intuition

As with many skills the basics of inquiry are easily learnt, but the adept phases take more discipline to acquire. Your own body, your emotions and mind are the instruments being used. Therefore the ability to amplify, to create or focus on certain states of mind and body are necessary. Your own wishes and fantasies can easily shift or shape what emerges in your awareness. Doubts about your ability to reach into the unlimited dimension of mind can shut the door completely to any result, so being able to quieten your mind is essential for the more refined and extended intuitive perception. However, a quiet mind does not mean one held so tight and immobile that no impressions can arise in it.

Similarly, the emotions and body need to be held in a receptive state – what has already been called the 'piano key' condition. Both of these are fundamental to the practice of inner-directed movement, but they need to be worked with even more consciously for extended perception. You need to develop the attitude of an observer without fixed opinions – on allowing a response to the question, and also in connection with whatever may be received. This freedom from opinion needs to be something you can take on when you choose to, and as with quietness of mind, it does not need to be something

The state of mind or consciousness that we call normal is simply the one we experience most. In terms of evolution and education it is the one which has arisen because it offers the most survival value, or is culturally created – that is, it enables us to survive in or fit into society. None of these factors make normal awareness anything more than one of many possibilities. There is no reason to maintain this habitual state simply because circumstances have induced it.

rigid. It's value is in preventing you from taking the information received and accepting it as infallible – to do so would be to have an opinion in regard to it. By considering what emerges in a non-opinionated way, you can more readily assess its usefulness and relatedness in connection with the original question.

Learning From Your Wholeness

To get a good response from inquiry at a level more subtle than physical movement you will need to have practised inner-directed movement for some months. Then the subtle responses of your mind and energy will be ready to receive the delicate impressions from your wider unconscious.

Using inquiry is not a strange or unconventional practice. Your being is always responding to the people you meet, the events you live through in subtle feeling responses and intuitions. This is happening right now, as you read these words. Inquiry is simply taking time to listen to what is already happening inside you, and learning to improve your skill in becoming more aware of this facet of your life. As your experience of inner-directed movement grows, there will be a developing subtlety in what arises. Gradually your interior feeling senses will operate more fluidly. Your voice will be exercised and used spontaneously as will your body. So you will be able to speak, sing, cry the depths of your being. In this way, when you make an inquiry, you will not depend on purely physical mime, but you may receive answers through mental imagery and insight, through shifts in your subtle feelings and sensations, or through the spontaneous expression of your voice.

Here are the useful stages of approach to inquiry.

1 If you are very fluid in using inner-directed movement you will not need a special setting in which to use inquiry; you could do it walking along a busy street talking with a friend. It is only during the early stages that you may need exterior help. For instance, some people using their intuition need cards, or to look at someone's hands. So if this is the first time you are using inquiry, prepare your environment in the same way as before.

2 Clarify your question. The wider awareness you are approaching responds most fully when you have a sincere need.

3 Ask the question and open your being to respond as fully as you are able. Be ready for the response to move you physically, sexually, emotionally, mentally and vocally. In other words, allow your whole being to be receptive. Observe what arises in a similar manner to watching a television screen when viewing a good film – that is, let the story, the plot, or the information, explain itself. Do not at this stage try to shape or question it.

> There are many forms of communication – mime, drama, emotions, words, imagery and fantasy, and combinations of these. The more you can allow your body, voice, emotions and mind to freely express themselves, the more this dialogue, this exchange, can take place.

4 Note the information you receive by writing it down or talking into a tape recorder. Once the response has unfolded its theme – the mime of the body movements; the story of the fantasy; the statement of your vocalisation – then work with the response, asking questions to clarify the subject until you are clear in your understanding of what is being received.

5 Consider what you have received and weigh it against practical observation. See if there is something you can learn from it and apply. Test it wherever practical. Do not be afraid to doubt it and try it against the world. If you are not accessing the best in yourself you need to know. This avoids the trap of wanting intuition to work at any cost. Intuition is a valid way of gaining information, just as your senses are, or your ability to read. But your senses and your ability to read are also ways in which false information can be taken in, so your discrimination is just as necessary when using your intuition as it is in everyday life. That said, do try not to fall into the trap of allowing discrimination to act as a source of doubt that blocks your ability to receive spontaneous movements and impressions. The more you practise it the sharper your intuitive judgement will become.

Chapter Five

Achieving Spontaneity

The Peaks of Experience

Knowing the viewpoint of other people in other times educates our own understanding. A summary of some of the other approaches to inner-directed movement will now be given in more detail than in the earlier chapters.

Seitai – The Open Approach

Seitai is one of the most open of the approaches mentioned here. It is non-religious, and is based on the simple observation of its founder, Haruchika Noguchi, that we have in us the power to stay healthy, or be healed if ill. This power of keeping balance amidst the changing forces around us such as heat and cold, trouble and calm, is the power of life that has formed our body. This power, which Noguchi saw as the self-regulating action of the body, can be influenced by the way one thinks and feels, by one's beliefs.

Noguchi has pointed out that if one feels confident about maintaining one's health, even though others are sick with colds or flu, then the body will remain healthy. This confidence in one's own power over sickness is seen as one of the rewards of using the movements. Confidence arises, Seitai practitioners say, because through the spontaneous movements you become aware of how the Ki – the energy of the living being – is released from its blocks in you, and can be directed more consciously.

As Seitai has developed from the Japanese system of thought, a mixture of Buddhism and Shintoism, it does not speak of any source of life outside oneself. But Ki is here the equivalent of the Christian Holy Spirit, or the Hindu Shakti – the force that shapes us and supports our continued existence. Seitai describes this as inherent in the person, but often mismanaged through negative mental attitudes and beliefs.

The Seitai practitioners I met were less pretentious about their method than individuals in other approaches I had come across. I was allowed to walk in or out of their practice as easily as one would visit a public swimming baths, and they had the same easy enjoyment of it. With stricter belief systems there is less freedom of behaviour and dress.

Availability

Unlike some of the other approaches, Seitai is unfortunately not yet a world-wide organisation. But considering its accessibility and open viewpoint, and the fact that it is such a safe and easy approach, and easy to practise alone or start your own group, this may well change. Its belief system and theory are so minimal it is difficult to go wrong in one's use of it.

Cost

The practice was always made available to me freely in Japan, though when attending a group led by a practitioner there are small costs connected with hiring a hall. This practice does not have a profit-making motive.

Contact

The headquarters of the organisation are: Seitai Kyokai, 9-7 Seta 1 Chome, Setagaya-ku, Tokyo, Japan.

The Work of Dr Wilhelm Reich

Reich was not only qualified in biology, as a medical doctor he also studied psychoanalysis under Freud. In the 1920s, he began to break from the Freudian school as he felt there was a more direct way to work with people through their body. He observed that the people who came to him always exhibited muscular tension in various parts of their body. Working with these he found that when the person was able to release these tensions spontaneous movements arose. These movements, so like Mesmer's early findings, were seen to be part of the psychosomatic healing process working automatically.

Reich observed that during this release there were often feelings of great streaming or energy in the person, sometimes linked with emotion and insight. Perhaps more than any other clinical therapist or doctor of his time, he recognised that a spontaneous, self-regulating activity or energy was at work in all living organisms. This, he observed, lay behind all of life's most important drives, such as breathing, sexual feelings, care and love. If this energy, which he felt was universal, was blocked in the individual, instead of flowing freely in their life as pleasure, sensitivity and a natural care and morality, it led to aggressive and unfeeling activity. He saw this behind the political and religious activities of his time, in which individuals counted so little.

Gradually Reich developed very definite techniques, working with respiration, muscular tension and character attitudes. He particularly explored the place of sexuality in individual, social and political structures. He helped people to release their own self-regulatory process and work with it toward health and wholeness. As people learnt this they experienced spontaneous movement, trembling, changed feeling states and emotional and sexual release.

Reich's influence has been enormous, but not on the established medical or psychological schools. Mostly his work has been taken up and extended by practitioners working under the umbrella of Humanistic Psychology or the Human Potential movement. Although spontaneous movement is still a strong feature in the work of people using his approach – now called Bioenergetics – there are a lot of psychotherapeutic theories and techniques in use, so there would not be a specific group practice.

AVAILABILITY

Easily found in most European or North American areas.

Cost

This varies. It is usually a led activity and so the group leader requires a fee. When used individually, as with a therapist, the costs are highest, often being between £15 to £30 per hour.

Contact

As there are so many groups and approaches to Reichian work, I am not able to give contacts that will lead to particular groups or practitioners.

Humanistic Psychology Practitioners
Ian Lee
14 Mornington Grove
London E3 4NS
Telephone: 081 983 1492

Self And Society Magazine
Editor David Jones
39 Blenkarne Road
London SW11 6HZ
Telephone: 071 228 1107

Human Potential Magazine
5 Layton Road
London N1 0PX
Telephone: 071 354 5792

These last two magazines feature articles and advertisements that give contact points.

The Subud Brotherhood

The practice of inner-directed movement within Subud is called latihan. It was founded by a man named Mohammed Subuh, an Indonesian. As Indonesia is largely Muslim, latihan has a slightly different theoretical base than the Charismatic Movement and

Shaktipat. It is, though, still seen as an action of the 'One great life' upon the physical and mental nature of men and women.

Much of the Indonesian viewpoint is built into the way the groups operate. For instance, one must not watch someone of the opposite sex practise their latihan.

Outside of Indonesia there is a three-month waiting period for new members, to ascertain their sincerity. Men and women are segregated during the latihan. Practitioners meet twice a week for about half an hour. There are no teachings with the latihan, as it is purely experiential. The monotheistic concept of Islam is a strong element in the approach to latihan, although support and sociability form a large part of the group experience, and most members do not push the Islamic aspect at all.

The long-term effects are said to cleanse human nature of forces that deplete free will. The major change is a growing sense of unity with the force behind all nature. Being Muslim, Pak Subuh calls this an alignment with the will of God.

Pak Subuh is called a helper rather than a guru, and there is no need to offer him respect or adulation. In forming the structure of the organisation he has made an obvious effort to make the latihan available to people of other cultures. Perhaps his great breakthrough was to offer it outside of a particular religious affiliation, although his innate cultural beliefs are still very evident. Pak Subuh also makes very clear his views on the cause of much human misery, namely dependence upon exterior objects for happiness.

The format of the practice, in which a group directly gives itself to spontaneous movement, makes it less obstructed by belief systems and ritual than some other approaches. Only Seitai manages to have an even more open door, standing as it does outside of any affiliation or direct connection with a teacher or group.

Subud, like Seitai, has a very direct practice of inner-directed movement. If you can deal with the limitations arising from Pak Subuh's belief structure − such as limiting the latihan to half an hour, men and women segregated, and the aim of the group being almost entirely a spiritual one, then this is an excellent way to use inner-directed movement.

AVAILABILITY

Nearly every large town has a group.

COST

This is not a profit-making organisation. Usually, about £2 a week is asked to cover the cost of hiring a hall, etc.

CONTACT

The official address of Subud for general enquiries is

Subud Centre
Watton Villa
Brecon
Powys
Wales
Telephone: 0874 623310

For local groups you should be able to locate a member's telephone number under the listing 'Subud'.

MESMER – FOUNDER OF MODERN SELF-HELP

Franz Anton Mesmer was one of the first people to observe inner-directed movement and explain it outside of religious beliefs. Around 1775 Mesmer, a qualified doctor three times over, began to experiment with magnets. He saw that 'incurable' patients could be healed through the use of magnets. He found that while people relaxed with magnets on their bodies, spontaneous or involuntary movements would occur. If these were allowed to be expressed strongly, the person would often experience healing of psychosomatic illness.

For a year he experimented with magnets in quite extraordinary ways. But within that period he realised the same healing results could be obtained without using them. He found that simply by stroking or touching the patient along the line of the nerves, the muscles would begin to twitch. This twitching, he said, should not cause alarm, even if it led, as it usually did, to an intensification of the patient's symptoms or even powerful movements. Throughout these releases, noisy and explosive though they were, he saw how patients could experience a healing of the distressing symptoms.

Mesmer is a transforming link with our own times because his approach to this phenomenon was an experimental and evaluative one. Nevertheless he was still bound to the past by his belief that another human being's presence was necessary to act as a channel for cosmic energy to reach the sick person.

Stefan Zweig, in his book *Mental Healers*, describes Mesmer's way of working as follows: 'With a serious and dignified mien, calmly, slowly, radiating tranquillity he would draw near to the patients. At his proximity a gentle fit of trembling would spread through the assembly. He wore a lilac robe, thus calling up the image of a Zoroastrian or Indian magician.'

Three hundred years ago, despite his exotic dress and manner, Mesmer ran what was obviously individual and group therapy of a successful nature. Although he thought of himself as a channel for cosmic energy, he nevertheless recognised an agent other than personal technical skill at work. Mesmer gradually moved into greater and greater complications, however – people dancing around trees, for instance – instead of simplification and clarity. Out of it came *Mesmerism* which took the form of positive suggestion, completely leaving behind the aspect of allowing the person to experience their own spontaneous process. Unfortunately, this rejection of the spontaneous, and replacing it with ritualistic or controlled activity, is a recurring theme. In Mesmerism – which became hypnotism – the spontaneous forces of self healing were usually ignored and even suppressed. The vainglorious power or forceful skill of the mesmerist or therapist took its place.

Nevertheless, a great deal of research has been done through hypnotism that relates to inner-directed movement. Great historical figures like Andrew Jackson Davies and Edgar Cayce, both of whom exhibited extraordinary ability in extending awareness, show the amazing possibilities of the human mind. Both Davies and Cayce could give information about people's physical condition without examining them, or even seeing them. (See *There is a River* by Thomas

Sugrue, Dell Publishing, USA, and *Edgar Cayce: Seer out of Season* by Harmon Hartzell Bro, Aquarian.) Although hypnosis can be extremely unreliable, 'peak experiences' can often be achieved with the right subject.

Mesmer's work has only been carried forward as hypnotherapy. Therefore no data is given about availability, etc.

THE WISDOM OF CARL JUNG

In *Psychological Commentary On The Tibetan Book of The Great Liberation* (ed. W.Y. Evans-Wentz, Oxford University Press), Jung says: 'If we snatch these things – experience of the world of the psyche – directly from the East, we have merely indulged our Western acquisitiveness, confirming yet again that "everything good is outside" whence it has to be fetched and pumped into our barren souls. It seems to me we have really learned something from the East when we understand that the psyche contains riches enough without having to be primed from outside, and when we feel capable of evolving out of ourselves with or without divine grace. . . . We must get at the Eastern values from within and not from without, seeking them in ourselves, in the unconscious. Because of these resistances we doubt the very thing that seems so obvious to the East, namely, the SELF LIBERATING POWER OF THE INTROVERTED MIND. This aspect of the mind is practically unknown to the West, though it forms the most important component of the unconscious.'

In Jung we find something of the reverence for what is met within a human being – a reverence for life itself – our personal power to find wholeness, and transcend our own limitations. One of his many great contributions is to see the 'self liberating power of the introverted mind' as being a natural process in us. It is not splitting hairs to say that his view of the transforming influence belonging to oneself, rather than being a gift from God or the work of magic forces, is in itself liberating. It is unifying. It heals the splits or conflicts created by seeing human and spiritual life as separate – one as insignificant and the other great. In fact, Jung points out in the same commentary, that one of the ills of the Western mind is its affliction with the idea that 'Grace comes from elsewhere; at all events from outside'. He goes on to say,

'Hence it is quite understandable why the human psyche is suffering from undervaluation. . . . For him – the western individual – man is small inside.'

Although it is not widely recognised, Jung did directly encourage his clients to explore spontaneous physical movement as a means to knowing themselves more fully. He explains his method in his commentary to *The Secret Of The Golden Flower* (trans. Wilhelm, Routledge, Kegan and Paul), a Chinese book about meditation. He suggests that one allows one's hands fantasy and play. In this way the unconscious can express itself despite the common blocks the conscious logical mind may set up.

THE ENLIGHTENMENT INTENSIVE

During the explosion of new or improved self-help techniques that emerged in the 1960s, Charles Berner started teaching a modification of an age-old form of Eastern meditation. The approach was very well known, and Kipling describes it in his book *Kim*. It was also the method recommended by the sage Ramana Maharshi. It is simply to ask oneself the question 'Who am I?' This was usually done alone, and took possibly years to carry the meditation through the surface layers of self to a direct experience of one's fundamental nature. Berner discovered that by working with a partner the results of this technique were speeded up to an unbelievable degree. The results were that one uncovered and experienced who one really was, beyond surface doubts and uncertainties. Berner called this technique Enlightenment Intensive.

Although Enlightenment Intensives do not start from the point of free-flowing movement, I see them as connected to inner-directed movement because they directly allow the same *process* to work. They encourage an open, allowing state of mind that allows whatever you truly are in yourself to emerge and be known. When that emerges in the process it does become strong feeling and movement.

The format is very simple. A group of people work together. You sit opposite a partner who asks a question which you have already chosen to work with. The question can be 'Tell me who you are', or 'Tell me what you are'. After making an intention to have a direct experience of who or what you are, take note of what you experience each moment, and report it to your partner.

It is stressed that you keep an open, allowing state of mind. When I experience this technique I was reminded of a vacuum cleaner. The open state of mind resembles a vacuum that sucks up any debris lying around and so cleanses one of attitudes and concepts that have been lying around for ages.

This is the total practice, but its simplicity hides a great deal of value. Although it may sound very cerebral – that one sits and responds to a question – in fact the thinking mind is transcended. At times the body is powerfully affected, along with the emotions. This is why I list it here as a resource for people using inner-directed movement.

AVAILABILITY

Practised as an intensive process over several days. This means it is an occasional event rather than an on-going practice. Therefore, availability depends upon whether you are near to an Intensive. These are not frequent, but are reasonably accessible.

COSTS

Fairly expensive because it needs to use of premises and helpers over several days. I paid £140 for three days, inclusive of food and lodging. The unwaged can get a lower price.

CONTACT

In the UK
Jake and Eva Chapman
The Old Manor House
The Green
Hanslope
Bucks MK19 7LS
Telephone: 0908 510548

Jan Adamson
CAER, Rosemerryn
Lamorna
Penzance
Cornwall TR19 6BN
Telephone: 0736 810530

Jean Whielden
Llanarrow
Huntingdon
Kington HR5 3QA
Telephone: 04973 439

In the USA
Dawn Nelson
20 Swan City
Walnut Creek
California 95496

The Charismatic or Pentecostal Movements

One of the best-known traditional approaches to inner-directed movement in our own culture is that which lies at the roots of Christianity. In reading Acts of the Apostles in the New Testament, in which the experience of Pentecost is described, a definite impression of a group practising inner-directed movement is given. The group had an open, allowing state of mind by surrendering to what to them was a holy influence – the Spirit. They also openly expressed themselves vocally in what is called tongues. This is not a rational singing of a hymn or song with known words. It is the expression of irrational sounds freely flowing, sometimes beautiful, sometimes harsh. Movement was also a part of the experience, so much so that they are said to have been thought of as drunk while they were allowing the spirit to move them.

Because of the sense of wonder and awareness of harmony between oneself and the rest of nature that occurs during some phases of inner-directed movement, it is not surprising, given that past cultures tended to explain natural phenomena in religious terms, that their explanation of the event was god-centred.

What is of great interest, however, is that the experience was seen as a healing and cleansing one. It was one that led the participants to feel great joy. They felt it to be so important that they wanted to communicate it to others.

As time went by, the freedom and spontaneity went out of the practice and became ritualised ceremony and stated dogma. Today the Pentecostal experience is being once again revived under the name of the Charismatic Movement. Because it is still strictly within a Christian belief structure, it may only be useful to Christians who want a freer and more joyous way of expressing their faith. My experience of it is that, like other approaches within strict rules of behaviour, there is a self-limiting factor to it that sometimes causes people to miss discovering some of the important dimensions of themselves which would be possible through inner-directed movement.

AVAILABILITY

Most towns have a church given to the Pentecostal approach.

COSTS

Usually based on donations.

CONTACT

Assemblies of God Headquarters
106/114 Talbot Street
Nottingham NG1 5GH
Telephone: 0602 474 525

Elim Pentecostal Church Headquarters
PO Box 38
Cheltenham
Gloucestershire GL50 3HN
Telephone: 0242 519904

SHAKTIPAT – THE INDIAN APPROACH

The word Shakti is Sanskrit. It refers to movement and energy, as does the English word 'shake'.

The practice is described as a letting-go of one's conscious ego enough to let an internal energy flow freely through one's body and mind. In the Indian tradition the original release is seen as arising through contact with a guru, although this is not an absolute rule. As the energy begins to flow the practitioner begins to move spontaneously, doing postures they had perhaps never done before, and singing in ways they had not practised or known previously.

These movements and sounds are known as kriyas. They might occur while the person is practising alone, but group practice is also used.

I do not have a great deal of experience with this approach. From what I have observed there is a very strong Hindu religious and yoga belief system surrounding shaktipat. The guru is of great importance. Before the kriyas begin, a great deal of chanting is used, so it is not so directly movement-centred as some of the other approaches described here. But I have seen a photograph of a large group of people, perhaps a hundred of more, using shaktipat in the open air. It appeared to be directly movement-based.

AVAILABILITY

There are centres in most Western countries, and of course in India.

COST

Although attendance at a centre is not costly – I stayed at the Ashram in Ganeshpuri for £2 per night inclusive of two meals – attendance of courses can be very expensive.

Contact

Gurudev
Siddha Peeth
Pin 401602
Ganeshpuri
District Thana
Maharashtra
India

Siddha Yoga Centre
Conford Park House
Conford
Nr. Liphook
Hants GU30 7QP
Telephone: 0428 725130

SYDA Foundation
New York
NY 12779
USA

Summary of the Approaches to Inner-directed Movement

In summarising what has been said about the various approaches to inner-directed movement, I am brought back to the very first paragraph in the Introduction to this book. Inner-directed movement is about RELAXATION. By letting go of physical tensions and rigid attitudes or anxieties, we free ourselves for fuller, more confident expression. We allow what Jung calls the self-liberating power. By opening more fully to its activity we express aspects of ourselves that were only potentials beforehand.

My own belief is that behind all the phenomena that arise from inner-directed movement, there lies a simple natural process. Just as self-regulation is the most likely force behind the movements and spontaneous experience, I see the potency of individuation behind the varied phenomena. By individuation I mean the action that moves us toward growing up physically and mentally. It is especially noticeable during our childhood and teenage years, but we see it at work throughout life as we mature. This growth expresses not only as powerful physiological processes but also as dynamic psychological forces. As such it links with the process behind dreaming and fantasy that is an intimate and important part of psychological growth and change. I believe this is why the apparently fantastic – deeply moving subjective experience and myth-building – is so frequently a part of this process of maturing.

I am not, however, saying there is nothing extraordinary or magical about these forces in us. Of course they are natural and a vital part of everyone's life, but the natural is not bounded by materialistic views. Our individual life is inextricably interwoven with our local environment, the world and the cosmos. We are a part of the ecological process. We can never be separate.

I do not believe that interior intuition or vision of nature's secrets is a supernatural process. A very large part is due to the mind's ability to scan huge amounts of information and experience and see them as a whole, as patterns or structures. Therefore, the very ordinary experiences and memories we have of walking down a street, of seeing our family and friends in their everyday experience of life, of witnessing the seasons, of being involved in change, are all crammed with information. When all the tiny pieces are put together we see certain cycles, certain processes working at all levels of existence. In this way we glimpse the powers of nature, of Life, touching the world and our personal existence.

While the older or God-centred approaches to inner-directed movement deal mostly with the personal relationship of oneself with the whole and with society, the more modern approaches explain more about one's relationship with oneself. So Mesmer, Jung and Reich have a great deal to say about psychological processes that act as barriers to the person finding peace and satisfaction. They believe that by working with the natural in the person, by stopping personal conscious effort and, as Jung put it, 'letting things happen' without interference, one can grow beyond previously insoluble problems.

Our awareness of being a separate individual rests upon an immense and ancient structure. Our being stretches right the way back from the conscious sense of self through the unconscious organ functions of our body, beyond the cells and molecules, into the atomic and subatomic to the mystery of what we have yet to find out about the foundations of life. Even if we never know all, there is certainly the possibility of meeting with that wonderful essence of life that is in every aspect of ourselves; the essence that is totally ourselves.

THE SIMPLICITY OF LETTING GO NEEDS WORKING AT

Profound subtleties lie behind the simplicity of letting go and letting things happen. Many of the tensions or character attitudes that hold us back are unconscious. A simple test on seven or eight people will demonstrate this. Ask a friend to sit in a chair, hands relaxed on their lap, and tell them you are going to move their hands and arms. Tell them you are going to do the work, so there is no need for them to make any effort. Then gently take one of their hands and support the arm at the elbow with your other hand. Slowly move their hand and arm, noticing how much resistance there is in their arm, how much they unconsciously try to help you. You will find in some subjects an uncontrollable urge to do the movements themselves, creating resistances. In many people the tension in their arms will be so strong that, if you take your hands away, their arm or arms will remain suspended in the air through unconscious tension.

The person whose arms you moved will feel quite relaxed, they will certainly not be aware that they had tensions sufficient to suspend an arm for quite a long period. These powerful tensions run throughout the body and are especially noticeable in the arms, legs, neck and jaw. Because they are unconscious they are not under voluntary control. If one is not aware of these tensions one does not know how to let go of them. The same test can be used on the legs and the neck. If the person has learnt inner-directed movement, and can allow spontaneous movement or response of feelings, a melting of the
can take place.

Having worked with people who have massive unconscious tensions in their muscles, I have found it is not simply a matter of pointing them out and the person relaxing them. What Reich found was that such tensions only melted when the emotional or attitudinal energy involved in them is discharged through movement and expressed emotions. It may take years to melt such tensions one by one through inner-directed movement. As each one is unlocked, so the energy used to hold it in place for years and the energy it restrained from expression are now available for your everyday use and enjoyment.

What Is Attainable?

To say what is realistically attainable is difficult because each person is unique. Some people never learn to swim, others swim the English Channel easily. The range of possibilities is enormous.

However, a fuller maturity is attainable. A dictionary definition of the word maturity is 'full development'. It means you can more fully develop those qualities and abilities that are innately yours, but may not have previously emerged.

Part of this maturity or full development is also self-responsibility. People who are used to blaming God, their parents, the government, their spouse, for their situation, gradually find their own power to change their lives and their characters. This is not always an easy transformation, because it is, after all, convenient to blame someone else.

Maturity may mean being capable of love or giving oneself to someone else. It may mean being easy and at peace with sex, or coming to terms with the world and people as they are instead of how our fear or prejudice might wish them. It can mean feeling comfortable with technology and religion, yet also wanting to produce positive change in the world.

In the end it is simply about being able to live your life as fully as you can.

Chapter Six

Your Internal Magic

The Peaks of Experience

When you allow your body to 'play' with possible movements and feelings; when you allow your emotions to flow and stretch themselves through their huge range; when you unleash your mind to soar and swoop amidst its immense territory of memory and experience; when you permit the unknown in you to move, recognise itself and cry out its song, you stand upon the very peaks of your experience. This is your wholeness knowing itself. This is the wonder of inner-directed movement. When these experiences come again and again, you will know them as the greatest moments in your life. They are moments that will add their colour to all that comes afterwards.

Getting the Best Out of Your Practice

One of the central secrets of inner-directed movement is the waiting. The act of waiting for your being to declare itself spontaneously holds a key that unlocks a fullness of experience which is otherwise missing.

The waiting, the spontaneity and the fullness of experience are intermeshed. Understanding them enables you to find the greatest satisfaction in yourself through inner-directed movement. If you miss this point you may experience creative movement, or improvisation dance, or movement to music – but you will not be experiencing inner-directed movement.

When you experience yourself as a seed growing, or as the element of water, or express yourself in the open approach, the end result is not just a pleasant period of physical movement. If it were, this book might just as well be called *Movement to Music*.

If you were only a body that might be enough. You are more than just a mass of chemical and biological processes. You have emotions, you have hopes and fears. You are an integral part of all you see around you as external. You are the wonder of life.

When you open to the totality of yourself and allow its expression you will experience excitement. You will know that more of yourself than usual is involved in what is happening to you. Much of what emerges will be unexpected and creative.

If, having used the graded approaches described, you have not felt that excitement, not touched the unexpected, there is still more for you to discover. But if you have felt the magic, there is no end to it. It continues forever, creative and new, though you bathe in it a thousand times.

USING YOUR ABILITY TO RELAX

The power to reach into your unconscious resources takes more than determination. To achieve it the conscious mind needs to become quiet and receptive. I am not suggesting that the passive, receptive state of mind is superior to dynamic, focussed will. However, each is an aspect of our total range of mental functions. Each accesses different possibilities or processes. Having one without the other is as incomplete as having an accelerator pedal without a brake on a car: although these functions are totally at odds with each other, they are both necessary. The ability to become passive and yielding is as vitally necessary as being active and resolute if we are to be whole.

The power of this state of mind has been observed by men and women in other cultures for thousands of years. Its importance has been recognised as so great that the yielding or quiet soul has been depicted as of supreme importance in seeking personal healing and enlightenment. This mental condition has frequently been symbolised as a holy virgin, the mother of God.

Joseph Campbell says in his book *Myths To Live By* (Bantam): 'There are myths and legends of the Virgin Birth, of Incarnations, Deaths and Resurrections; Second Comings, Judgements and the rest, in all the tions. And since such images stem from the psyche, they psyche. They tell us of its structure, its order, and its forces, c terms.'

If your experience of inner-directed movement is already spontaneous and creative, then you already know how to open, or yield. If not, use the approach in which simulated yawning is allowed to lead into spontaneous yawns and movements until you feel at ease with the unwilled movements your body makes. Also try the experiment of pushing your arm against the wall and allowing it to rise by itself. Don't discard whatever level of response you get in the practice. Carry on and enjoy it, letting a little more yielding enter it as you gain trust in yourself.

> Remember that inner-directed movements do not usually start with a thunder clap of power that overrules your own will. They arise gently, almost imperceptibly. By allowing the tiny urges to move, like the almost imperceptible impulse to breathe while your body is quiet, the movements get stronger and more power flows.

HELP IF YOU CANNOT LET GO

Sometimes a major tension gets in the way of being able to let spontaneous movement happen. Three special techniques might be useful. They are not to be used on the same day, but separately, and as you have need.

Help Method One
Give yourself up to half an hour for this – shorter or longer as your needs dictate.

1 If you are aware of tension in yourself, allow it to become stronger. Be willing to experience it deeply.

2 Do this by standing in your 'space' as usual, with appropriate music playing. Take time to really feel the tension and allow it to direct your body posture, feelings and any movements.

3 The tension may get worse as it is discharged, so be prepared for this. It is perfectly natural.

Help Method Two

Prepare your space with fairly active music. Plan to give up to an hour to this. Keep the music playing for that length of time.

1 Move, or dance, to the music in any way that you can. It doesn't matter how awkward you feel, how stiff, how much resistance you have to this – DO IT! Keep going no matter what, until you can feel the blocks or tensions melting and easy spontaneous movement emerging.

2 You may need more than one session to break through the physical tensions, fears and emotions that imprison you.

In his book *Black Butterfly*, Richard Moss describes the experience of an elderly woman, dying of cancer, who was taking part in his spontaneous movement class. The woman was supposed to be dancing freely to the music, but was hardly moving. When he asked her why, she said it was because of her illness. He said to her, 'You are not dead yet – move'. She did so and to her amazement the movements got easier and she experienced a shift of awareness in which she realised she was an unseparated part of an ocean of life. Her physical illness was totally healed.

Help Method Three

Instead of movement you can use your voice. Take about fifteen to thirty minutes for this. Use quiet background music as an aid to giving yourself permission to make sounds, but be careful of pushing your voice too far as you may become hoarse.

1 Stand with eyes closed. Become aware of your breathing rhythm. Slowly deepen it but do not speed it up. If anything, make it slower and fuller.

2 When you feel at ease with this add a sound to the outbreath. It is easiest to use the *aaaaahhhh* sound at first.

3 Keep this going until you feel the sound flowing out easily and

reasonably smoothly. Then move the sound around by changing the volume. Make it soft, make it loud. Try the different volumes of your voice and the different levels of power.

4 Next, try shifting the feeling quality. Make different sounds to see what variety of feelings you can discover or express. If you hit a satisfying sound, something you can enjoy, move it to express laughter, change it into sadness, thoughtfulness, anger, hurt – in fact try it in all sorts of pitches and feeling qualities.

5 This can be very entertaining because the voice is an incredible instrument, so enjoy yourself with the instrument you have been playing since babyhood. If words find their way into what you are doing let them – but see what range of feelings you can express with them.

6 When you have finished playing the instrument of your voice, relax quietly on the floor for a minute or so. This quiet period after the voice exercise is often very healing. It can produce very real internal peace.

Some Results of Inner-directed Movement

Some of the body's ways of self-regulation are not comfortable. Some people do not like sneezing or vomiting. Yet these uncomfortable movements are necessary at times to help keep the balance in your being. Such cleansing, not only of the body, but also of the emotions, is occasionally a part of inner-directed movement. An 'emotional sneeze' might rid you of an emotion such as guilt or grief that you are unconsciously holding onto and is causing stress in your body – just as a physical sneeze gets rid of harmful dust or bacteria. In Seitai, it is emphasised that at the beginning of the practice the body may discharge toxins that have been harboured for many years. Therefore the practitioner might perspire more heavily than usual. Sometimes a mass of mucous is discharged from the nose during a practice. Noguchi also says that occasionally a person even sees something like a piece of glass come out of their body after having existed there for years from an injury. Quite rarely, but worth mentioning, an old scar or mark from long past might show on the body again for a short period as the effects of past shock or hurt are dispelled. More commonly, however, we are cleansed of negative emotions and memories during the practice.

The overall action of inner-directed movement appears to lead towards a reasonable level of wholeness. That is, the opposites of one's nature are allowed expression until they find balance. The healing processes in the body are made more efficient, and it attempts to do what I call the backlog of 'housework'. That is, old feelings we may have been holding onto to our detriment are discharged.

Once the physical and mental housework is done, then the process moves toward integrating and reviewing your life experience, to draw out of it what lessons, insights and creative ideas you have gathered. Some of the Eastern practices see this as a spiritual change in which one becomes more aware of one's links with the rest of nature.

YOU HAVE MANY SENSES

When your mind, voice and emotions are allowed expression alongside your body movements, as occurs spontaneously during inner-directed movement, something very special happens. Old patterns of movement, behaviour and emotions are played out during practice. Then gradually new or creative forms of expression arise. You break through the old patterns to discover a wider, fuller you.

As you emerge from these restrictions, you will find that your ability to see what is going on around you deepens. Your senses are not restricted to sight, touch, hearing, taste and smell.

Very often the full range of our emotions have not opened. This is largely because muscular stiffness, physical tension, emotional injuries from the past, keep us from fully responding to each moment of experience. As one's body becomes more mobile; as emotional debris is cleared; as old rigid concepts are cleared from the mind, new levels of sensation arise.

When we are still cluttered with old hurts or rigid feelings, we may see the physical movements of people and animals; we may see the light reflected from their bodies, we might feel whether they are warm or cold, wet or dry, and experience their perfume – but we would fail altogether to see or understand what motivates, moves, impels or disturbs them. We would not perceive their emotions. Their state of mind and body would not be visible to us. We might not deeply experience our kinship with them.

What You Can Gain

Colin explains this from his own personal experience of inner-directed movement.

> To understand what a change came about in me you must realise that for all my teenage years I was painfully shy. I remember that even at fifteen when the whole school assembled each morning to sing a hymn, I found it painful to be visible in such a large group of people. I wasn't standing in front of everyone. I was just mixed in with my class. Nevertheless it was agony.
>
> Inner-directed movement has helped me let go of some of those feelings that had haunted me since those years. Even though I didn't use music as a background to the practice, I found myself doing a lot of stamping dances. To me it felt just as if I had been taught some Red Indian tribal dance. I was chanting to the movements too. And there was a lot of power in stamping. It made me feel strong physically and emotionally. I had never before in my life made those sort of movements or felt those feelings. Somehow they enlarged me, because beforehand I didn't know I had it in me.
>
> At one time the dance movements were more African. I remember the pleasure that I felt when, like an African chief calling to the tribe, I roused them through my movements and chanting. The power in my voice was such that I boomed out feelings and commands with intense emotion. It was a wonderful experience to feel my body filled with strength and self assurance. It was almost as good as having lived it, so the feelings were ones I can now find in my everyday life. My son was still a baby at the time and I found I began to hold him differently. I felt my own body communicating strength and enjoyment of life to him – maybe even reverence of life. Sometimes during practice I had even felt what seemed to me the way I felt as a baby, and from this I was able to relate more fully to my small son.
>
> Other things I did during the practice had helped me experience the

flow of love through me, and this has become a part of the way I relate to other people too. Not only do I feel it in myself, but from the experience of it I can see it operating in other people, even in animals. Sometimes I will see it pouring out of the eyes of a mother with her child, or in the face and posture of a couple. If they catch my eye a sort of instant recognition occurs. They know I have shared what they are experiencing and they smile.

What Colin is saying is that until he had experienced certain emotions or feelings he could not see them in other people or in nature. Once his repertoire or range of experience had been enlarged, there was a lot more to see and connect with in the world.

In an article on inner-directed movement ('Rituals of Beauty – Awake in a Dream', *Harpers and Queen* September 1984), Leslie Kenton says:

> Often, as a result of trauma, life stress and social or family situations which are not naturally supportive of individual growth and development, we become separated from our own feeling sense or we tend to relegate it to the level of insignificance. When this happens, one's life tends to become strongly habitual, mechanical, and eventually largely unsatisfying, no matter what kind of worldly success, excitement and glitter it may contain. For any real sense of joy, satisfaction or meaning can only come when the inner and outer being are linked up and when what Crisp calls the feeling sense is allowed the freedom to regulate both physiological and psychological processes.

Inner-directed movements help you develop an extended repertoire of physical expression. Because the body and personality are united, this means you have a greater range of responses to other people and events, and a greater awareness of what you see around you.

SEXUALITY

To give an idea of how inner-directed movement relates to sex, it is helpful to think of how a plant puts forth its sexuality – its flower. The flower is produced only at a certain point in the growth or cycle of the plant, and is usually very different in shape and colour to the leaves or stem. The visual experience of watching a plant form a small bud that gradually grows and opens into a flower is exciting. The process is vulnerable, though. If you think of something interfering with the flowering, inhibiting it at some level, then the flower exists, perhaps only as potential, but is not yet functioning fully.

The complex opening of human personality and sexuality has some kinship with this. Certain aspects of it can easily be inhibited in their flowering, or the spontaneous instincts which usually inform and shape their growth are withheld, suppressed, turned away from their task and full opening. Because inner-directed movement builds a link between your natural inner life and your conscious self, any aspects of your possible growth which have not emerged may be allowed. This does not happen overnight, but it is a wonderful possibility. In fact, few of us can reach maturity without some aspect of our nature, whether sexual, emotional or mental, being left behind, hurt or perhaps not given enough attention because other areas of activity were demanded by the needs of the time.

THE MIND AND EMOTIONS

After some weeks of teaching a group, Julie told me that something new had come into her life from what we had been practising. She said, 'I never knew before that I have an inner life. This is such a wonderful thing for me.'

My understanding of what Julie was telling me was that she had never previously known what riches of experience and creativity, of insight and perception she already owned. She had thought of herself as just another housewife and mother, not unintelligent, but an unimportant person among billions of other unremarkable people living and dying.

The treasure Julie found that can be discovered through inner-directed movement is not to be mistaken with the realisation of intelligence or personal ability. A young and brilliant college student was recently describing to me his own realisation of his inner life through this practice. He said:

I know this may sound strange, but the most powerful thing for me was that I realised I am alive. The realisation was accompanied by the sense of being life. I now know I am life and life is not just a chemical reaction or a set of biological drives or responses. As life I am always exploring, reaching out, becoming, learning what I am capable of and what I am. Just to exist is itself a great pleasure and miracle.

As with Julie, Len's realisation during inner-directed movement was not about his own intellectual ability or personal value. He had already proved his intellectual brilliance and ability in his scholastic performance. This had not given him the sense of being alive and liberated though. The contact with his own vital inner life enabled him to realise he was more than he thought he was. He learned through his own experience that the essential part of himself did not begin or end with his body, his emotions or his thoughts. From this arose a sense of freedom and liberation he had not known before.

Len's changed experience of life was the result of just a few sessions of inner-directed movement using the open approach. Previously, he had been very reticent in relationships, yet often felt lonely. As he learned to let his own love shine out, he found it easier to make friends. He says:

At first I found it difficult to let go enough for my body to freely express itself. When I did learn to do this my movements were very strong. At the time I was lying on my bed because my movements had started from quietness and stillness. They became so strong I fell off the bed at one point. My impression was that without realising it I had been holding back enormous amounts of my own energy. It was when I let the full current of my energy be expressed that I could achieve a new experience of myself. It is like having a dimmer switch on a light in an internal room, and all the time you have it just glimmering, and the room looks dark and dismal. Then one day you turn the power up and the whole room is transformed. All the colours glow, and features not seen before stand out.

For many people this sort of release only occurs in times of crisis, high emotion, or if they are challenged by a public appearance. At other times the dimming effect of social or intellectual conditioning, anxieties, or not knowing how to let go, make us feel less than we really are. In fact you are more than you have ever believed.

Touching this vastness brings with it a sense of great wonder. In a recent letter to me, Len describes what he feels when he touches what he calls 'life' through inner-directed movement.

> When I remember life and cry, as I am now, it is not sadness, it is everything. It is the beauty, the tragedy, the joy, the vastness, the thrill, the miracle, the mystery. It is a love from the depths of life of all creatures who have the courage to love, to embrace life in its vastness. From the firefly flashing its statement to the night, or the sparrow fetching worms for its young, to the dog running with joy toward me.

Inner-directed movement gives you access to a new and vital experience of yourself outside the patterns of emotion and trains of thought from which you usually erect your self-image. It leads to a discovery of your own unique inner life more fully than most forms of meditation or mental disciplines.

You Are Life – Live It

Apart from the sort of experience Len described, there is already a remarkable dimension of yourself which you may be overlooking. It may not seem important, yet many people who use inner-directed movement learn to see it as a doorway of hope.

It can be explained by imagining a scene in the long past. You are on a primeval river bed looking at the thick mud on the banks and gazing at the semi-tropical plants and trees. As you watch, a small deer is pursued by a prehistoric human being. The ancient human hunter runs after the animal across the mud leaving evident footprints.

The day has passed, the mud has dried, another day has begun. The hunter comes back to the river bank. With the caution necessary in this untamed environment he approaches the river and drinks. As he straightens and turns to go he notices the baked footprints. He follows their line with evident excitement. You sense he is reading the prints and feeling again the emotions written into the fluid movements now baked dry and preserved. He puts his feet into the prints and a look of strangeness comes onto his face. You share this magical moment with him as for the first time he realises his individual existence and feels with an almost painful emotion that he is looking back at himself in the footprints.

He looks down at his body, his hands, his feet, seeing them for the first time in this new light of self-awareness. Then he walks slowly to where there is still wet mud. Purposefully he places his foot in the mud, removes it and looks at the result, making a sound as an animal might as it declares its existence during mating. He again places his foot in the mud, and twice more, until the four prints make a cross, with the large toe of each print at the centre. He stands staring for a long time, oblivious of his surroundings, in awe at what he has done.

This scene is not pure fantasy. Something like it must have occurred at the dawn of history. It portrays the life of the instinctive animal, already on the verge of a new kind of awareness, crossing the threshold to self-awareness for the first time. Until that point all the actions, all the reactions, all the inner life of that creature arose out of instinctive drives or group information. All actions were performed in relation to some real need such as hunger, mating, running from danger. The threshold was the realisation that an action can be performed for no external need at all. It can be done for no reason other than curiosity, play, an exercise of mind. And so the first work of art arose – the first imprints in the mud that were not the result of the hunter chasing the animal, or running for safety, but just because!

Until that moment the human animal could only live within very marked boundaries. The footprint in the mud stepped completely beyond those boundaries. It was freedom after millions of years of unconsciousness and instinctive behaviour. It was an open door to an infinite variety of action and feeling. It was frightening and disturbing because freedom means no set rules, the unknown, the yet to be. It was stupendous.

It is impossible to describe all the implications of the 'cross of footprints'. Without it we would be imprisoned within certain restricted reactions to our environment. Our response would be limited to what we had inherited through our instincts and possibly learnt through painful experience. Human beings have a massive potential intelligence, but many of us are still extraordinarily limited in our repertoire of behavioural responses. We still haven't quite taken in the fantastic meaning of art and music. We still haven't really read the message left on the wall by the cave dweller who painted an outline of his hand, or fashioned the image of a bison, or who created symbols and ideas of gods and God, or pissed a pattern in the snow.

> The message reads – I have found a new freedom. I have become more than I was. I am the creator.

Perhaps it is because we have developed a cultural attitude that splits things up, separates body and mind, spirit and flesh, that we find it difficult at first to believe such freedom, such realisation, can come about by allowing the body to move and express itself freely. Life is not a series of compartments. Our being is an integrated whole. If you allow your body freedom of movement, to go beyond what it has done before, then you are allowing your mind and emotions to do the same. You have gone beyond yourself. You have transcended what you were.

Of course the footprints in the mud story is just an example. But whatever it was that led human beings to paint, imagine, behave in ways that were outside of the necessary survival behaviour, also opened the door to music, variety, drama, freedom of the senses and rigid roles. It means that a person with a broken body need not have a broken soul. They are limited only by their ability to imagine and experience. We are no longer limited by being born a certain sex, or by our own or other people's ideas.

> You are an integral part of a whole. Life is not trying to control or destroy you. You can take your place within the scheme of things if you wish. Your connection with the whole is through your own intuitive response to life. You can find this by allowing the spontaneous in you to emerge and declare itself. Then you will see for yourself that from the cosmic viewpoint the opposites of life and death do not have the same importance you attach to them while you only see life through your physical senses.

THE SPIRIT

The film *E.T.* captures our heart and imagination because it depicts our own longing to find a connection with life beyond our physical limitations. It is a story about being trapped and dying in an alien environment. *E.T.* elicits longings in us to share the life of something beyond Earth.

This lost creature from a wider life, a more inclusive life, a more powerful life, a more connected life, is lost, trapped and injured here on Earth. The film brings out our longing for a connection with life that transcends time, space and death. It is a desire for wholeness.

> People frequently describe the essence of what they find through inner-directed movement as touching life itself, as the life-force, as something which enables them to be free of things that shackled them, or that healed them of major illness. If this wonderful fount is given the name spirit, then in meeting your spirit you will always find more of yourself.

Inner-directed movement is a progression towards greater freedom from bonds; liberation from the monsters of self-doubt, dependence on a partner or a social role, or guilt and rigid rules and beliefs. It opens you to the transforming influence of the spirit. It allows you to be touched by a power to heal sickness. If anything, this freedom, this move towards independence, this healing, is the real spiritual jewel to be found as your being liberates itself.

The movements you allow and the energy of your life – life itself – reveal your innate freedom. There is no goal in this practice, and that in itself is a freedom. The moment your body gives expression to its own needs you have cast off one of the great bonds – social pressure to conform. You will find level after level of freedom beyond that, each with its own reward and difficulty. For freedom requires responsibility, and it means losing chains that may have become precious in some way: the loss of beliefs previously cherished; the falling away of opinions that gave strength of purpose; the removal of walls of defence against meeting people and against your own fuller experience. There is a way of experiencing life which only unveils itself to you if you dare to unrobe your mind and heart, if you chance the adventure of freedom from your own fears, and if the only reward you seek is that of liberation from your self-imposed limitations.

DARING TO LIVE YOUR BEST

Two years ago I watched a young man leave college showing obvious signs of anxiety about his own abilities. His offhandedness about authority also suggested he feared from the outset he would not receive help from any organisation. Despite having many gifts, and being highly intelligent and imaginative, he nevertheless suffered a great deal of despondency about himself and how inadequate he felt. The world around him appeared to cause a degree of anxiety that paralysed him.

During my attempt to understand what held him back and what his potential was, my intuition presented me with the image of a young bird on the verge of leaving the nest. What struck me when I considered the idea was that the bird had in fact never flown before. It had no experience of flying. There was no way of practising before it took that amazing leap into the literal unknown.

The small, unskilled, inexperienced bird takes the leap, dares death, opens its wings and flies – because a greater, older bird, a wiser, experienced creature stands within the small one. Perhaps you would give it the name instinct. Whatever you call it, the unequipped immature bird, by its very leap, calls upon the experience of flight lying dormant in itself. The Great Bird, the ancient experience, would never come to the small juvenile bird if it had not made the leap. If you don't take to the air you will never learn to fly. If you never plunge into the water you will never learn to swim.

In humans this wiser, more experienced self is our dormant potential. Dr Clair King accepted the reality of this potential when he was confronted by a child with an injured eye. Five-year-old Robert Kasner was taken to him for an emergency eye operation. His cornea had been slashed by a piece of flying glass, allowing the liquid in the eye to drain out. The operation was performed at Aultman Hospital, and a flap of conjunctiva pulled to patch the wound. After twelve days the dressing was removed, only to reveal that the patch had not held. The iris was protruding again. Robert needed another operation. An appointment was made for three days later.

When Dr King examined Robert prior to the second operation he could not believe what he saw. The eye was completely healed. He was astonished, even embarrassed. On asking the parents how this was possible, they told him simply, 'We took Robert to a Kathryn Kuhlman service. Prayers were offered for his healing.' (*God Can Do It Again* by Kathryn Kuhlman, Oliphants) Dr King Later joined the Order of St. Luke the Physician.

> You have the power to access healing changes. You have a reservoir of potential from which you bring treasures to your everyday life. If you are ill, it is possible to reach into this unconscious storehouse and find healing change. If you are empty of pleasure you can be filled. If you are dead inside, you can come to life. I know that even if you do not trust enough to let go fully and find a fast miracle, you can certainly allow a slow miracle to take place.

USING YOUR INTUITION

The unconscious often reveals intuitive knowledge. The relationship between the young, inexperienced bird and the Great Bird is certainly intuitive. The word 'intuition' is defined as knowledge not gained by reasoning and intelligence. It can also be seen as the gaining of information or perception without the use of our usual senses. We each have enormous powers of intuition if we accept the above definitions.

Intuition is not acclaimed in the work-a-day world as a practical and useful ability. Perhaps if your situation or work are routine and unchallenging, then intuition may have no real use for you. But if you are involved in the uncertainties of life and work; if you are faced with previously unmet situations in your relationships or your projects, you need every resource you can access.

Betty describes an experience of this everyday side of intuition.

Daniel, my son, was in the middle of studying for his A levels and was facing a lot of uncertainty. The amount of effort and commitment needed was very great, but also he was having to make decisions about what direction to take in his studies that he realised would influence the rest of his life. He kept asking himself and me whether he was making the right decisions. We had talked around the subject a lot, exploring the various possibilities. So it wasn't that we hadn't given time and thought to the subject that was maintaining the question for Daniel.

One evening we were sitting in his bedroom and again the question arose. I said to him, 'Look, we've talked over this lots, and going over the same things again aren't going to give us anything new. I would like to talk to you from another part of myself just to see if it is any more helpful. Daniel knew I used inner-directed movement, and I explained to him that I had found it often gave me unexpected and useful new views of things – did he want to hear what might arise from that source? He said he did.

I had discovered that if I gave myself permission to be moved from within, words and images poured up into consciousness without me having to think about them. So I sat with my eyes closed in this way and asked the question of what would be the most useful direction for Daniel. Within moments I started speaking – and you have to understand that I didn't know what I was going to come out with, so I felt some tension as to what I might say to Dan; would it be stupid or banal? What I said was something like this. 'There is a story about a young man. He was setting out on a journey by himself. He hoped to reach a town some miles away. He had only walked a few miles when he came across a fork in the road. He hadn't realised when he had started that he might not know the way. He knew where he wanted to get, but he didn't know now which road would be the right one. There were no signposts to say, and he must decide without help. He stood there a long time struggling with the problem. But try as he might, he could find no clues as to which road would lead him to the town. If he took the wrong one he might go so far from his destination much time would be lost. So he was unable to move. What he didn't know was that it didn't matter what road he took. Further on the two roads linked again so both led to his destination'.

I was amazed that I could make up a story about Dan's situation without any conscious effort at all. But also, that I could so unhesitatingly tell him the story. The important thing for me was the effect hearing it had on him. It appeared to bring alive a truth he already knew in himself. The change was very quick. He never needed to talk about choices again. That was some years back, and he still talks about decisions in a way, telling me the story is now a part of the way he thinks.

Let your time of inner-directed movement be an opening to the wisdom you have within yourself. Do not limit yourself. Neither you, nor anyone else yet, know the limits of human ability and experience. There is nothing in this practice apart from the discovery of who and what you are. If you live with doubts or limited views about yourself, that may seem a very small gain. But those who have made the journey encourage you to open to the discovery of the many dimensions of yourself still left to find. Becoming yourself in fullness will be the greatest adventure of your life.

INDEX